CATHEDRALS OF THE SPIRIT

CATHEDRALS

OF THE

SPIRIT

The Message of Sacred Places

T. C. McLuhan

HarperPerennial
HarperCollins*PublishersLtd*

First Edition

Designed by Nancy Singer

Canadian Cataloguing in Publication Data

McLuhan, T. C.
Cathedrals of the spirit

ISBN 0-00-638033-6

1. Sacred space.   2. Sacred space - Pictorial works.
3. Nature - Religious aspects.   4. Nature - Religious aspects - Pictorial works.
I. Title.

BL580.M35 1996   291.3'5   C95-932437-2

96 97 98 99 ❖ RRD 10 9 8 7 6 5 4 3 2 1

Printed and bound in the United States

To my mother
Corinne Lewis McLuhan
. . . of untold grace . . .

CONTENTS

I'm too religious to believe in religion. You don't have to believe in a sacred world. It slaps you in the face. It's everywhere.

AN EIGHTY-YEAR-OLD HUNGARIAN FRIEND
TO GRETEL EHRLICH, POET AND NOVELIST[1]

As soon as you look at the world through an ideology you are finished. No reality fits an ideology. Life is beyond that. That is why people are always searching for a meaning to life. . . . Meaning is only found when you go beyond meaning. Life only makes sense when you perceive it as mystery and it makes no sense to the conceptualizing mind.

ANTHONY DE MELLO (1931–1986),
INDIAN JESUIT AND SCHOLAR[2]

We all move on the fringes of eternity and are sometimes granted vistas through the fabric of illusion.

ANSEL ADAMS (1902–1984), PHOTOGRAPHER[3]

The more I think about this mystery [the metamorphosis of the earth], the more it appears to me, in my dreams, as a "turning-about" of consciousness—as an eruption of interior life—as an ecstasy. . . . Spirit has only to be reversed, to move into a different zone, for the whole shape of the world immediately to be changed.

PIERRE TEILHARD DE CHARDIN (1881–1955),
PALEONTOLOGIST AND JESUIT PHILOSOPHER[4]

This entire cosmos, whatever is still or moving, is pervaded by the divine.

ISA UPANISHAD, THE VEDANTA,
ANCIENT HINDU SCRIPTURES (CA. 2500 B.C.)[5]

The third millennium will be spiritual or there will be no third millennium.

ANDRÉ MALRAUX (1901–1976),
ATHEIST, FRENCH POLITICIAN AND WRITER[6]

ACKNOWLEDGMENTS

I am greatly indebted to the New York Public Library for the privileges of the Wertheim Study, a refuge of dream and creation for my writing endeavors of the past twelve years.

The interlibrary loan services of the library have also been invaluable in their facilitation of the broad research that is the backbone of a book of this nature. Philip Yockey, Jane Greenlaw and Robert Dumont have been particularly helpful in tracking down elusive titles and material. I am most grateful to them for their goodwill, resourcefulness and, most importantly, their good humor. To Wayne Furman, Office of Special Collections, I express my appreciation for the courtesies granted by his office and his continuing interest in my work.

I wish to thank John Lundquist, Chief Librarian of the Oriental Division of the library, who has introduced me to the intricacies of that collection—a goldmine of cosmic knowledge—and who has guided me in the expedient use of its substantial resources which are inexpendable to a book such as this one.

I extend my gratitude to Executive Editor Larry Ashmead for his encouragement and unfailing appreciation of my efforts. To Associate Editor Jason Kaufman I owe my thanks for his thoughtful comments and enthusiasm throughout the writing of the book.

And Loretta Barrett, my agent, has been a source of unwavering support that has contributed greatly to the realization of the book.

INTRODUCTION

This book is about sacred places. It is about landscapes of the holy as centers of inspiration where human consciousness is temporarily set free. The experience of a sacred place and thus sacredness itself is re-entry into a state of wholeness—an introduction to your true origins. Hence the goal of this book is to reintroduce you to yourself.

Sacred sites are ancient, holy, living repositories of the sacred images, eternal truths, physical, social, and spiritual needs as well as the profoundly human potential of numerous traditional cultures across the planet. Within the context of our own economic criteria, "most sacred sites," writes anthropologist Fred Myers, "are said, therefore, to be 'gold.'"

Sacred places are revered the world over. They are often identified as natural sites such as trees, mountain peaks, moors, waterfalls, hillocks, isolated rock outcrops, water holes, caves, forests, springs, the environs of burial mounds. Apart from these naturally occurring sites, there are places of sanctity crafted by human hands: granite monuments such as dolmens (mushroomlike structures made from slabs of stones), the megalithic stones of Carnac in

Brittany, Stonehenge on Salisbury Plain, underground chambers like the King's Chamber in the Great Pyramid and the Native American kivas of the Southwest; stone wells such as Chalice Well at Glastonbury in southwest England, Great Serpent Mound near Peebles, Ohio, and the Great Temple at Machu Picchu in Peru; the rock galleries—"open-air Louvres" as they've been called—scattered across Aboriginal Australia and Africa, to name a few. These holy places reveal spiritual laws, encourage social and cultural cohesion, express the significance of attachment to place, and help determine the quality of life.

Sacred landscapes are but one dimension of the mysterious and the holy. These spiritual centers of the earth are distinctive in their supernal nature. The word *sacred* means "holy," and the terms *holiness* and *health* are from a Germanic root word that means "whole." The early Christian mystics referred to the quest for wholeness as the way of "oneing." Ralph Waldo Emerson perceived sacredness and its place in the fabric of the universe as a metaphysical expression of humankind's highest potential. "Nothing at last is sacred," he wrote, "but the integrity of your own mind."[1] *Integrity* derives from the Latin *integritas*, which means "wholeness," "completeness," "purity." "Man is a god in ruins," Emerson stated, whose ultimate aspiration is a reintegration of the fractured human spirit. As loci of rememberment, sacred sites are engaged in the "drama of *being*," writes one Kiowa sage, and therefore must be carefully protected. They are also timeless paths to the very heart of human existence.

From Chartres to Aachen

Cathedrals of the Spirit offers a cross-cultural mapping of human consciousness as it plumbs the significance of a multitude of sacred sites through the revelations of those who have experienced and imagined them. The deeper currents of energy that illuminate and unite humanity are a prominent feature of this exploration. The most sacred site of all in Western mythology might easily be considered "heaven," and the vehicle of transport, the cathedral. The word *cathedral* derives from the Greek word *cathedra,* which means "seat," "throne," "author-ity." (A cathedral differs from a church in having a bishop's chair, called a *cathe-dra.*) Standing in a great medieval cathedral, a person may feel on high, as it were, or at the center of the world. The traditional sense of cathedral-as-edifice is expanded here to include arboreal cathedrals, underground, Stone Age and cathedrals immemorial, open-air cathedrals, and the cathedrals within.

The magnificent Gothic cathedrals of the Middle Ages were important pil-grimage centers that celebrated worldly ideas of the celestial spheres. The Church of Saint Denis near Paris, for example, became a burial place of kings and the French national sanctuary. Chartres, the quintessential Gothic cathe-dral—built between 1194 and 1220—was designed by an unknown master according to the sacred principles of ancient astronomy and geometry. The entire structure of the cathedral is encoded with the perennial wisdom of the ancients. Its renowned Pilgrim's Labyrinth of black stone, drawn on the floor of the nave under the rose window (and an exact reflection of its diameter), is but one concrete symbol of the sacred architecture that signifies passage into another world, a return to the source. In fact, the prevailing medieval expression for "labyrinth" was "Road to Jerusalem," the route to the *omphalos,* the center or navel of the earth.

The late-eighth-century cathedral of Aachen in West Germany, built by Charlemagne, is yet another example of ancient knowledge recharged and incor-porated into its heavenly proportions. Paul Devereux, a leading authority on geomancy, reports that its Palace Chapel, built on the plan of the octagon and the oldest part of the cathedral, possesses exceptional astronomical properties that result in the equivalent of sunbeam fireworks. Devereux noted that a strik-ing affinity with the latitudinal alignments of the ancient imposing megalithic forms of Stonehenge, Avebury, and the Great Pyramid emerged not only from the octagonal blueprint of the Palace Chapel but also from the kaleidoscopic patterns of sunlight.[2]

The Very Reverend James Parks Morton, dean of the immense Gothic

Cathedral of Saint John the Divine in New York, writes that cathedrals "by their very nature" were built to represent the entire world. "They are microcosms . . . a vision of the Heavenly City right here on Planet Earth. The harmony of inter-connectedness that we call Peace (or Shalom or Salaam or Mir) is meant to be visible before our eyes."[3]

Footprints of Heaven

A meeting of the heavens and the minds of the great monument builders under-scored the architectural admixture of the human and the divine. The beauty and splendor of ecclesiastical sacred spaces invoked celestial expressions of a par-adise to come. Nothing was spared to encourage exaltation and transport into heaven on earth. Sublime stained-glass windows, the proliferation of precious gems and gold that embellished the tabernacle, crucifixes, chalices, shrines, and the sumptuous robes worn by the clergy were a true manifestation of a terres-trial heaven. Awe-inspiring architecture, angelic singing, supernatural light, stately processions of silk and ceremony combined and conspired to catapult both laity and clergy into the divine realm of the heavenly Jerusalem. The Gothic cathedral was an impressive realization of the popular medieval image of heaven. The cathedral construct is clearly a persuasive metaphor, profoundly moving and satisfying. Today, perhaps, there is less pomp, circumstance, ritual, and fewer communicants due to the increased secularization of ceremony and a flourishing of modern pilgrims seeking less traveled paths to the deeper mean-ing of life. *Cathedrals of the Spirit* considers other approaches to—and interpre-tations and expressions of—"heaven" and paradisiacal space.

The Benedictine monk and author John Main (1926–1982) once stated, "The Kingdom is not a place we are going to but rather an experience we carry within us on every breath." Saint Catherine of Siena (1347–1380), who once spent three years in silent meditation and was called "the mother of thousands of souls," said, "All the way to Heaven is Heaven." Similarly, the very spirit of

Zen reveals the accessibility of divinity through the common miracle of every moment, every day. In this context, I am reminded of Mahatma Gandhi's response to an inquisitive reporter who wanted to know why and how he worked so committedly. Because, he replied, "I am always on vacation."

Bernard of Clairvaux, a dominant spiritual personality of twelfth-century Europe, found "heaven" in the book of nature. He saw nature as an allegory of heavenly things. His understanding of the reality of the divine sciences and Holy Scripture came from the pageantry of the woods and fields. "I have had no other Masters than the beeches and the oaks," he wrote.[4] A Catholic encyclopedia defines heaven this way: "the place and state of perfect and eternal happiness. It consists primarily in the sight of God face to face, termed the Beatific Vision: this sight involves the spiritual possession of him and the love of him to the utmost of the creature's power."[5] Buddha speaks of nirvana as "the highest happiness." The unknown, illumined writer of the ancient Hindu epic poem, the *Mahabharata*, states: "The devotee, whose happiness is within himself, and whose light (of knowledge) also is within himself, becoming one with the Brahman, obtains the Brahmic bliss." In Dante's *Divine Comedy*, Beatrice is cosmic happiness itself. Dante describes the radiant Love that is Beatrice: "That which I was seeing seemed to me a smile of the universe; for my inebriation was entering through the hearing and through the sight. O joy! O ineffable gladness! O life entire of love and of peace! O riches secure, without longing!"[6]

Almost every page of Walt Whitman's *Leaves of Grass* bears testimony to the happiness and loveliness contained in the inner wonders of union with spirit: "Wandering, amazed at my own lightness and glee," writes Whitman. And "O the joy of my spirit—it is uncaged—it darts like lightning." Finally: "The ocean filled with joy—the atmosphere all joy!/Joy, joy in freedom, worship, love! Joy in the ecstasy of life."[7]

So much joy. How can we know this place and state that summons up such expressions of exaltation and divinity? What is the meaning of this unified experience of Being? *Cathedrals of the Spirit* invokes the landscape of sacred places—man-made, natural, and divine—for insight and foresight into the riddle of human existence.

THE CALL OF SACRED PLACES

"Sacred place . . . is a construction of the imagination that affirms the independence of the holy," writes theologian Belden C. Lane.[8] Divining the sacred in *loca sacra*, in other words, is essentially an initiation into sanctified space that is autonomic in its revelatory capacity. "In actual fact, the place is never 'chosen' by man," says historian of religions Mircea Eliade. "It is merely discovered by him. . . . [T]he sacred place in some way or another reveals itself to him."[9] Indeed, the ancient Greeks referred to sacred locales as *abaton*, inaccessible ground. The notion that holy ground chooses rather than is chosen constitutes the core of innumerable spiritual traditions across the planet. What's more, pioneering Swiss psychologist Jean Piaget believed that a very young child lives in a world of perpetual grace in that it is instinctively aware of the patterns of divine insight. He wrote that "the child behaves as if nature were charged with purpose." The idea of a "completely profane world," adds Eliade, "the wholly desacralized cosmos, is a recent discovery in the history of the human spirit."[10]

The dynamics of sacredness and holy space is most vividly characterized by those unique individuals who spontaneously know they have never been separate from its life-affirming power. Their voices reflect the perennial knowledge of ageless traditions that are inseverably linked to the unified ground of Creation. Islamic sage and Malian humanist Amadou Hampate Ba reports that "the deepest secrets of life are hidden in the bowels and tunnels of the earth. Myth tells us that life began in a grotto, grew in a well, and burst forth from a crevice."[11] When an Australian Aboriginal elder speaks of the billowing rock mound of Uluru in the desert of central Australia, he describes it as a sacred record of his people's ancient origins—no different from himself—possessing the magical powers of a magician's rod to evoke the land's ancestral energies. A Pitjantjatjara guardian of the living presence of this sanctified site expresses his inalienable linkage to the place with these words: "I am Ayers Rock. . . . This is my great ceremony . . . this holy cave . . . this great camp with its holy tree."[12] Land *is* self, "the very soul sustenance," writes Aboriginal poet, playwright, and artist Kevin Gilbert.[13]

Earth: Soil as Soul

The Havasupai Tribal Council chairman, Lee Marshall, describes the inherent makeup and function of land as a ground of being, as a vital and unifying element of Native American existence. The interaction of beliefs with the soil upon which they flourished and out of which they originated is an integral part of Native American thinking about reality. Marshall, whose people live in one of the great wonders of the world, the Grand Canyon—now a National Park Service "zoo"—once summed up U.S. Forest Service officials' discussions on the significance of the Grand Canyon to the Havasupai tribe with the following comment: "I heard all you people talking about the Grand Canyon. Well, you're looking at it. I *am* the Grand Canyon."[14]

The Black Mesa mountain range of the Arizona desert is a sacred universe to the Dine (Navajo) people. It is the flow of Creation itself: "Black Mesa begins in us. The Four Sacred Mountains are our laws. Navajo people emerged from the previous worlds, here, between our Four Sacred Mountains, and this is where we must remain to live in the Dineh-Navajo Way."[15] Nigerian scholar Cosmas Okechukwu perceives the whole earth as holy, and "since the whole earth is sacred," he writes, "every part therefore is sacred in a general way and is treated as such. So literally the people lived in the midst of the sacred."[16]

Japanese Zen Buddhist philosopher Daisetz Suzuki believes "the earth is man's very body." She is boundless love, a profound source of joy; the earth is humankind's "great educator" and "great disciplinarian." A person's own excellence is achieved because of her, states Suzuki.[17] Greek writer Kostas Pasagianis conveyed the experience of the "blue, mystical light" and "the thrice-blessed non-existence" of the mountain world of Greece where "deathless, incorruptible Life flourished" and "the mystery of the world's birth" is apprehended.[18]

Emerson viewed the far-seeing soul as self-aware, a knower of the unknowable, a "choral song which rises from all elements and all angels." He wrote, "Man is made of the same atoms as the world is, he shares the same impressions, predispositions, and destiny. When his mind is illuminated, when his heart is kind, he throws himself joyfully into the sublime order, and does, with knowledge, what the stones do by structure."[19]

THE NATURE OF SACRED PLACES

The nature of sacred places is comparable to the nature of the divine in that nothing is unrelated to them. Henry Miller wrote that "our destination is never a place, but rather a new way of looking at things." In this regard, acknowledging the bountiful role of story, ritual, and myth in the sanctification of place,[20] consider, additionally, the following approaches to hallowed ground for a wider interpretation and understanding of the holistic significance of sacred landscape.

- Sacred places as perceptions of reality
- Sacred places as not merely locations but events where all time is eternal time
- Sacred places as sites for re-memberment
- Sacred places as renewed crucibles of consciousness
- Sacred places as encyclopedias of self-knowledge
- Sacred places as time capsules from ourselves to ourselves
- Sacred places as portals to ascent

- Sacred places as a geography of the imagination
- Sacred places as centers of reconciliation of the sacred and profane
- Sacred places as realms of recollection of things to come

Entering into a sacred landscape is an experience charged with human potential. The pilgrims who journey through the pages of this book attest to a fundamental creative and spiritual efflorescence that erupts *in situ*; in many instances, a recovery of a state of grace is conferred. The shared touchstone of these voyagers is an allegiance to the mystery of life.

ARBOREAL CATHEDRALS

Few are altogether deaf to the preaching of pine trees. Their sermons on the mountains go to our hearts and if people in general can be gotten to the woods even for once to hear the trees speak for themselves, all difficulties in the way of forest preservation would vanish.
John Muir (1838–1914),
naturalist and conservationist[21]

Trees are the oldest and largest life forms on earth. They cultivate our spirit and offer sustenance, solace, beauty, and shelter. Forests are much more than great congregations of trees. They are complex synthesizers of the fundamental elements of life. Trees play a unique and crucial role in the earth's great ecosystem—as vital laboratories that alchemize, with the help of the sun, water, air, and nutrients, into living matter. Were it not for forests, the earth's atmosphere could not be replenished and the planet's fresh air supply would not support the kind of life we know. Each and every tree, no matter how small, plays its part in this great planetwide drama of renewal. Many of us feel that something is amiss in a treeless landscape. Indeed, some people like to live in trees: A young New

Yorker went so far as to surreptitiously construct a series of thirteen elaborate tree houses in Central Park in which he lived for eight years until park police discovered and dismantled them. "Life is good in the trees," reported the unrepentant arboriphile.[22]

Cultures across the planet acknowledge the sacred and healing power of trees. Native North Americans think of trees as our teachers and elders; the boddhi tree of India is reputed to be that hallowed ground where Buddha received enlightenment; the baobabs of Africa are centers of ceremony, ritual, and medicinal knowledge; Abraham played host to angels under an oak; the sequoias and redwoods of the American West are now considered an incalculable national treasure and spiritual resource. The Chilula people, who have lived in the northern California redwood and pine forests for centuries, say that the redwoods are spirits incarnate. "The essence of the trees has a way of touching the inner soul of mankind," states tribal member Fido Davis. "Such an experience makes a person feel humble and secure. It gives meaning to our existence. That is why we say the Redwood forest is like a church; the trees have power and are alive."[23] And indeed, an Akuropon elder from Ghana reports that in times of war or crisis a chief was able "to turn himself into a tree" as a protective tactic.[24]

In his autobiography, Carl Jung encounters a tree of passage—the Tree of Life or Cosmic Tree (a universal symbol of the omphalos: the cosmic axis, the root of roots, the Divine Egg)—in one of his own dreams in the guise of a silky, heaven-scent magnolia, in which the importance of the omphalos in human development is finally confirmed for him. He relates that at the heart of his dream was a little island ablaze in sunlight, surrounded by soot and shadow. "On it stood a single tree," he writes, "a magnolia in a shower of reddish blossoms. It was as though the tree stood in the sunlight and were at the same time the source of light."[25] The great twelfth-century Rhineland mystic, theologian, and musician Hildegard of Bingen bequeathed us the term *viriditas*, or greening power. She talked and wrote of "the exquisite greening of trees and grasses" and how all of creation and humanity, in particular, is "showered with greening refreshment, the vitality to bear fruit."[26] William Blake wrote in 1799 that "Nature is imagination itself" to the human being who beholds imaginatively.

CATHEDRALS IMMEMORIAL

This cave simulates origins in a way that makes contemplation all
but unnecessary. In a sense, I have been left stranded at the entrance
to myself.

James Cowan, Australian poet and writer, in the
deeps of an Aboriginal sacred site[27]

Caves have been called "Stone Age cathedrals" and "vast underground natural temples." Since antiquity, shamans and animists have utilized caves as prime venues for their rites. The cave is a place of retreat, a ground for reconnection deep within the womb of Earth Mother. "It is in caves," writes Mircea Eliade, "that aspirants have their dreams and meet their helping spirits" during their initiation into shamanistic knowledge. Likewise, the kivas built by the Pueblo Indians of the American Southwest are, in effect, artificial caves, subterranean sanctuaries of stone, chambers where ritual and ceremony are practiced to this day.

The Paleolithic cave of Lascaux, discovered in the southwest of France in 1940, displays a range of paintings and drawings of animals that astonish in their power and beauty. It has been theorized that these profoundly moving images, vibrating in the darkness of a near inaccessible interior point, were the conduits to communing with the divine powers.[28] Certainly the difficult labyrinthine approach to the inmost recesses of the rock womb where the images are recorded and where encounters with Spirit may have transpired suggests the prevailing symbol of the timeless winding passage that is humankind's journey of ascent to the Divine Essence.

Equally, the 1994 find of the Chauvet cave near Avignon in the south of France—with its more than three hundred awe-inspiring, intact paintings and engravings estimated to be about twenty thousand years old—has revealed an altarlike set piece: the skull of a bear enthroned on a large rock in the middle of one gallery against a backdrop of bear paintings. One French expert has commented that "even the way animals are drawn . . . is evidence of something sacred."[29]

Caves of sanctity, of ceremony? Many archeologists have long believed that the deep prehistoric caves were places for illumination and enlightenment through the practice of shamanistic rituals. Even today, the Kogi, who call themselves the Elder Brothers of humanity and who live on an isolated dome-shaped mountain mass—the Sierra Nevada de Santa Marta in Colombia—begin the training of a *Mama* (enlightened one) in a cave at infancy.

The magnificent Stone Age caves of Lascaux, Chauvet, Trois Frères (in the Pyrenees), and Altamira (northern Spain) are thought to be the precursors of the great Neolithic chambered mounds such as Newgrange in Ireland, Gavrinis in Brittany, Maes Howe (the Orkney mainland, off the northeast coast of Scotland), and the underground Iron Age souterrains of northwest Europe. The celebrated quarter-mile-long serpent effigy and earthwork, Great Serpent Mound in Adams County, Ohio, should be mentioned here as well as the prehistoric Indian mounds of the upper Ohio River and its extensive tributary systems.

Later examples of sacred subterranean landscapes include the great fifth-century Chinese cave temples at Yunkang that consist of a series of spectacular sculptures of buddhas and boddhisattvas, heavenly musicians and swarming winged messengers, all carved out of a sandstone cliff in commemoration of the early kings of the northern Wei dynasty. A complex of cave shrines of equal splendor is Mahabalipuram near Madras in southern India, built by the seventh-century Pallava kings. A modern pilgrim, the monk and poet Thomas Merton, upon seeing Mahabalipuram, wrote: "[M]y Asian pilgrimage has become clear and purified itself."[30]

Earth revealed itself to me as a living being, and rock and clay were made transparent so that I saw lovelier and lordlier beings than I had known before, and was made partner in memory of mighty things, happenings in ages long sunken behind me. . . . The body of the Earth has special regions through which the traffic of perception seemed most clearly to take place.

George William Russell, Irish agriculturalist, nature mystic, and poet describing a dramatic shift in consciousness at a verdant sacred site, 1932[31]

Large rocky outcrops, hillocks, mountain peaks, the great stone megaliths, and rock galleries are regarded by many cultures as markers of the mind, seats of wisdom and perennial knowledge. Claude Kuwanijuama, a Hopi spiritual leader, has said that "man does not have the only memory. The stones remember. The earth remembers. If you know how to listen they will tell you many things."[32] Lone Man, a Teton Sioux, explained in 1918 that the earth was protected by a power that is sometimes manifested in the form of sacred stones, large and small. "The presence of a sacred stone," he pointed out, "will protect you from misfortune. *Wakan Tanka* tells the sacred stones many things which will happen to people."[33]

Saint Brynach, the celebrated sixth-century holy man, repeatedly experienced mind-expanding visions and communion with angels at Carn Ingli ("Hill of the Angels"), one of the peaks of Mynedd Preseli, a hill range in southwest Wales. The Irish writer George Russell received dazzling insights into "the memory of nature" and "the memory of Earth," which he could tune into at will on the hillsides outside Dublin and the sand dunes by the western sea. At these holy sites, revelations of "most ancient, ancient places and peoples, and landscapes lovely as the lost Eden" were made known to him.[34]

Equally, the fusion of man and mountain into a living embodiment of truth and light as the way to knowledge of self and the universe is a fundamental belief of many extant traditions. Mountains as metaphors for transcendent states of being, as living repositories of sacred energies and conduits of power and revelation, as sacred states of consciousness and as places of divine providence occupy a prominent position in the spiritual life of innumerable cultures across the planet. The thirteenth-century Japanese Zen master and teacher Dōgen tells us that "from time immemorial the mountains have been the dwelling place of the great sages; wise men and sages have all made the mountains their own chambers, their own body and mind."[35] The Kogi of Colombia, who make their home on a mountaintop, know that mountains are sacred and wise: "The Mother told us to look after all mountains. They are ceremonial houses. We know that all the mountains we see are alive. So we make offerings to them." And a Tewa prayer instructs that "within and around the mountains, your authority returns to you."[36]

The Way of Correspondence

Conscious, interactive landscapes were daily events in the lives of our ancestors. Traditional cultures the world over recognize this reality. The megalith builders of Stonehenge, Avebury, the Great Pyramid, Chaco Canyon, Machu Picchu, Teotihuacan, and Palenque constructed their sanctuaries according to the sacred principles of ancient astronomy and geometry based on the system of correspondence, the core of which was Nature. "The most ancient people," wrote the Swedish engineer, scientist, and mystic Emanuel Swedenborg, "were celestial men [who] thought from correspondence itself, as the angels do." Swedenborg defines correspondence as follows: "The whole natural world corresponds to the spiritual world, and not merely the natural world in general, but also every particular of it; and as a consequence every thing in the natural world that springs from the spiritual world is called a correspondent."[37] Swedenborg's thinking is congruent with Aboriginal wisdom and Islamic philosophy relating to the world of correlation. For instance, the Gagudju of Arnhem Land in northern Australia know that the maturing of the fiber on the pandanus tree is irrefutable proof of sharks in nearby waters giving birth to their young. The eleventh-century visionary Abu Hamid Muhammad al-Ghazzali has written that "the visible world was made to correspond to the world invisible and there is nothing in this world but is a symbol of something in that world."[38]

The megalith builders understood that the structures they were building were astrophysical sites, points of contact with the greater universes. They are time capsules containing "star mathematics." "The whole thing is very much . . . a beautiful and holy vision," wrote Thomas Merton of his pilgrimage to Polonnaruwa in Sri Lanka where the great stone buddhas stand and recline. When the Trappist monk felt strangely inarticulate about his experience of this divine place, an Indian colleague advised Merton: "Those who carved those statues were not ordinary men."[39]

The power inhering in these ancient monuments was real. The ancient builders were spiritual engineers who knew the way of the heavens and the principles of perennial truths. That sacred knowledge was a portal to a profound realization of the ineradicable connectedness of humankind with Earth, with its own divine essence and the cosmos beyond.

THE CATHEDRALS WITHIN

To acquire the awareness of the Divine, one need not journey to any special region or place. It is enough if the eye is turned inwards. In the Bhagavadgita, *the Inner Reality, the* Atma, *is described as "splendorous like a billion suns." But man has not become aware of the light and power within.*

Sri Sathya Sai Baba, Indian avatar[40]

In Teresa of Avila's *The Interior Castle*, the individual is a pilgrim who is travel-ing to an unknown destination where the human and divine merge. It is an inner journey marked by contemplative activity and interior footwork. As in all journeys, there are stages, plateaus, labyrinthine passages, obstacles, and unex-pected epiphanies. Voyaging through the seven dwelling places of Saint Teresa's clear crystal castle of the soul is both a spiritual and earthy adventure. Her citadel of many mansions is magnificently spacious "with lovely gardens and fountains and labyrinths, such delightful things that you would want to be dis-solved in praises of the great God who created the soul in His own image and likeness."[41] It is a pilgrimage of self-discovery; a call to completeness; a call of ascent. The great sages from time immemorial have explained that the meaning and purpose of every journey is to come home. Whether we are journeying across the sea to the Holy Land or to the sacred city of Mecca, traversing the road to Canterbury, Mount Koya, the plain of Arafat, Santiago de Compostella, or simply visiting a local shrine, meditating, or reaching for the invisible spiri-tual concourse inside the human soul, the journey is essentially the same—the journey to the Center.

How does one characterize a pilgrim? Theologian Richard Niebuhr does it this way: "Pilgrims are persons in motion—passing through territories not their own—seeking something we might call completion, or perhaps the word clarity will do as well, a goal to which only the spirit's compass points the way." Everyone becomes a pilgrim sooner or later, he writes, "even though we may not give ourselves the name. Words and their meanings are animated by cur-rents of energy . . . summoning us to be on our way."[42] The occasion that prompts the summons may be as varied as it is mysterious and magical. Matsuo Bashō, the seventeenth-century poet-pilgrim, described himself as "a travel-worn satchel," as he tumbled along the unknown paths of his eight-hundred-mile trek through the mountainous terrain of northern Japan.

The journey itself, the pilgrimage, takes many shapes and forms and is filled with myth and symbol. In India, the act of *tirtha-yatra*, "making pilgrimage," is considered the holiest of undertakings. Commitment to *tirtha* consitutes one of the highest expressions of faith in the divine mystery. The Hindu classic, the *Mahabharata*, charts 330 sacred places and rivers in a pilgrimage itinerary that crisscrosses the entire land of ancient Bharat. Richard Leviton, an authority on earth mysteries, describes his own pilgrimage as "autogeomythics—myself living the myth in the landscape." He writes, "every pilgrimage is self-reflexive and interior. You are the geography of the road . . . ; unflinching self-knowledge is the key to waking up. . . . Think of your whole life as a pilgrimage. Ever since you first asked the question—what is my life all about, anyway?—you have been making the pilgrimage toward an answer."[43] In her book *On Pilgrimage*, social activist Dorothy Day states that her whole life experience of living "here and now the life of the spirit" led her to the conviction that the main failing of humankind has been "not to love enough." She adds, "The *whole* person, the *holy* person must be the central actor in the new civilization."[44]

In *The Journey to the East*, Hermann Hesse writes of the universal metaphysical underpinnings of the quest for enlightenment:

> *I realized that I had joined a pilgrimage to the East, seemingly a*
> *definite and single pilgrimage—but in reality, in its broadest sense,*
> *this expedition to the East was not only mine now; this procession of*
> *believers and disciples had always and incessantly been moving*
> *towards the East, towards the Home of Light. Throughout the cen-*
> *turies it had been on the way, towards light and wonder, and each*
> *member, each group, indeed our whole host and its great pilgrimage,*
> *was only a wave in the eternal stream of human beings, of the eter-*
> *nal strivings of the human spirit towards the East, towards Home.*[45]

The anonymous spiritual classic *The Cloud of Unknowing* (probably late fourteenth century) refers to one stage of the journey as a "stark awareness of your own existence." It is a recognition "touched by the deepest existential sorrow," writes one twentieth-century monk, for we apprehend for the first time the true meaning of our inherent separation from Spirit, the duality that marks our human lesson. Transcendence of this existential sorrow into the fullness of the boundless joy of being is the heart of the journey homeward.

The practical, visionary, ecstatic, wise, transcendent, ceremonial, inquiring nature of landscapes of the sacred is glimpsed in the pages that follow. This chrestomathy speaks to the wonder of it all. In these evocative testimonials, the natural and sacred links between the cultures of the world are underscored, revealing the spiritual laws of our planet and the sacramental character of the universe.

Five years ago I discovered an enchanting photograph of a tree in an esoteric journal and intuitively put it aside, knowing that one day I would seek out its creator. Some time later, as *Cathedrals of the Spirit* was taking shape, I embarked on my search for Eliot Bowen, the photographer. It was a mission that consumed four months and involved a trail of dead-end addresses, bouts with various post offices, and legal assistance. Finally locating him and learning that he had other photographs, I traveled to rural Washington State to meet with him. Together we decided to explore the rain forest of Hoh in the Olympic Mountains of the Pacific Northwest. There we captured additional images for use in the book.

What drew me to Eliot Bowen's work was its engaging anthropomorphic and zoomorphic character—his ability to recognize and evoke human and animal forms in nature, especially in trees and megaliths. Such configurations are present in many mythologized landscapes across the world, but it takes a mythically sensitive eye to discern them. Understanding the symbolism of these metaphysical expressions of Nature is a process of awareness requiring a great depth of consciousness, which the voices in this book both reflect and address. Many ancient traditions are manifestations of this mode of being. For example, at the heart of Australian Aboriginal existence lies a towering compassion and exuberant affection for the land that animates its living presence and reciprocates the life-sustaining power of its eternal embrace. Nosepeg, a distinguished Pintupi elder from central Australia, explains that an outcrop of gigantic boulders are much more than simply rocks. "They were," he said, "an old man and his many wives who had huddled together for warmth from the cold southerly wind."[46] Every atom of their sacred landscape represents the embodiment of some ancestor, and its potential fertility is palpable.

The weathered "faces," figures, and animal forms that emerge from the trees and stones in Eliot's photographs could very well be spirits and deities making themselves known, suggests the photographer. On occasion, deep in the forest, desert, or other ancient site, he has felt their presence. If we can *see* the "faces" and shapes now, imagine what they were like before they were weathered!

Another attribute that attracted me to Eliot's pictures is a mysterious quality—indeed, the informing element of his work—produced in large measure by his innovative use of infrared film.

He explains that the shortest wavelength of light that humans can see is perceived as the color violet. Just beyond violet is ultraviolet, which we cannot see. At the other end of the visible range, the longest wavelength of light an individual can see is red. And the invisible light just below red in frequency is called infrared. While we can't sense infrared with our eyes, we feel it on our skin as heat. Specially designed films make use of this part of the invisible light spectrum.

"Infrared photographs are often described as having a dreamlike or surrealistic appearance," says Eliot, "due to the combined effects of the haloes and altered tonal relationships, which give them their distinctive look. Human skin and the surfaces of leaves can appear to have an unnatural glow, almost as if they were emitting light rather than reflecting it. It is interesting to me that infrared images are perceived as dreamlike, since the world of dreams and visions in a sense lies just beneath the visible range of our waking experience."[47]

One of the aspects of infrared film that most appeals to Eliot is its unpredictability and its capacity to reveal another layer of reality—one he cannot see. "I never really know what my pictures are going to look like until I print them," he says. "The dreamy and mysterious appearance of infrared photos is sometimes matched by the mystery of wondering how the pictures will look when they develop."

The layers of information that Eliot is inspired to expose in his photographs are those that reveal forms and shapes that he sees in nature—"which I think others don't often notice." With that as a goal, he says, color becomes a distracting element, so he prefers black-and-white film—most often black-and-white infrared film.

Photographing trees and rocks became a passion for Eliot at an early age. The faces in nature became natural occurrences; and the frequency of their appearance in his work burgeoned as his belief in the "omnipresence of consciousness in the natural world increased."

A large number of Eliot's arboreal photographs focus on the base of the tree. "This is the part of the tree," he believes, "that most often seems to reveal the tree's distinctive character. The lifelong struggle of a tree to survive in its chosen circumstance is recorded in the cracks, scars, and contorted surfaces at or near its base, in the same way that the lines, spots, wrinkles, and scars of a person's face record the joys and sorrows of a human lifetime."

The spiritual and whimsical impetus of Eliot's work is of particular appeal. His illumined approach to photographing the natural world has succeeded in challenging ordinary modes of observation and creating what Susan Sontag has elsewhere called "another habit of seeing." Landscapes, trees, and stones may never quite look or feel the same way again to those who have experienced his photographs.

The images that appear in the book span Central America, Europe, and North America, and were taken over the last seven years. The subjects of his pictures range from the giant redwood trees of northern California—"the yogis of the forest," as they've been called—and the impressive "totem" trees of the rain forest of Belize in Central America to the great megalithic sites of Stonehenge and Avebury in England and the mysterious standing stones and balancing rocks of Utah and Oregon. The healing, divinatory, and fecund properties of stones and sacred groves go back to the remotest of times. A number of the photographs in the book reflect the shapes that symbolize those virtues and powers.

ARBOREAL CATHEDRALS

Riverbanks lined with
  green willows, fragrant
  grasses:
A place not sacred?
  Where?

SAYINGS OF THE MASTERS[1]

When a man plants a tree, he plants himself.

JOHN MUIR (1838–1914),
NATURALIST AND CONSERVATIONIST[2]

Reclining Woman

*ustralian poet and author James Cowan returns to "the metaphysical terrain"
of Aboriginal Australia that he visited with his Aboriginal friends more than ten years
earlier. Using the epistolary form to recapitulate his journey into the "interworld" of the
Australian wilderness, Cowan gives an intimate portrait of a breathtaking universe
where, in the infinity of dimensions, the revelation of the sacred is made manifest.*

LET ME TELL YOU ABOUT A TREE under which I slept last night.
The baobab is like no other. Squat, bulbous, smooth-trunked impre-
sario with a penchant for accumulating water in the dry months, this
tree drops velvet-skinned pods as large as a man's fist. To awake in the
morning to the sight of such small hemispheres littering the earth is
to know one has been visited by Mimi Spirits. These are their baubles,
and the seed within them a clamour of echoes that suggest a fecundity
not always visible.

Mimi Spirits, you say? Well, how else am I to describe a visita-
tion by what is eternal? The baobab, after all, is a giant lingam, a phallus, filled with seminal substance. Leaning against its curvaceous
trunk, it's easy to regard these pods before me as the playthings of
spirits. More than once I have seen them on cave walls in the arms of
Mimi figures, ochrous gourds which, when emptied, become ideal
water carriers. Thus a man or spirit can journey afar in search of veri-
ties, knowing that in his pursuit of knowledge he will not die of
thirst.

Is this possible? My friend, Idumdum, seems to think so. He has
made many journeys in the footsteps of his forefathers during his life-

time, hoping to encounter their lingering presence among the rocks and caves of the region. When he asked me to accompany him on a seasonal visit to his country, I knew the privilege he wished to bestow upon me was one of collusion. You see, Idumdum had recognised in me a water carrier like himself. We were creatures of the baobab, seed bearers, men who longed to render what we saw and experienced as something more than temporal.

So what I want to speak of now is the Dream Journey. Idumdum has joined me in an excursion into the *alcheringa* [eternal time]. Much of what we have seen so far has a quality of revelation, in keeping with the idea that we have, in a sense, left the earth. . . . His country, I soon realized, was none other than a *spiritual universe* containing images supremely important to his well-being. . . .

Idumdum and his friends regard the earth, their land, as a celestial image. They are enamoured by its many categories of sacredness. For these possess their souls, transforming their habitat into the vision of an ideal iconography.[3]

Call of the Stones

*H*e was only nine years old when he renounced the world and joined the wandering brotherhood of Jain monks in India. At the age of eighteen, author, pilgrim, and peace activist Satish Kumar was dissuaded from this path by an inner voice and became a campaigner for land reform in a renewed India. In 1973 he settled in England. "It is an Indian tradition that when you are fifty you should go on a pilgrimage," writes Kumar, so in the summer of 1986 he walked to the holy places of Britain—Glastonbury, Canterbury, Lindisfarne, and Iona. In his autobiography, *No Destination*, he describes this ongoing remarkable journey that began in his childhood and gradually became the trigger for the inner odyssey of his maturing years. In the following passage, Kumar discovers the wisdom of a tree.

THE CHURCHES, CATHEDRALS, MOSQUES and synagogues, shrines and temples are not the only holy places, but the whole of creation is divine and sacred. My pilgrimage is in every moment and in every place.

Sometimes I came across a tree which seemed like a Buddha or a Jesus: loving, compassionate, still, unambitious, enlightened, in eternal meditation, giving pleasure to a pilgrim, shade to a cow, berries to a bird, beauty to its surroundings, health to its neighbours, branches for the fire, leaves to the soil, asking nothing in return, in total harmony with the wind and the rain. How much I can learn from a tree! The tree is my church, the tree is my temple, the tree is my *mantra*, the tree is my poem and my prayer.

Standing under a tree by the Gapping River, I realised that the law of nature is to create energy and life by uniting. A seed united with the soil creates the tree; water united with the earth produces crops. When man and woman are united in love, they create a child. Wherever there is unity, sacred and positive energy is generated.[4]

$\mathcal{M}$atsuo Bashō's eight-hundred-mile pilgrimage through some of the most rugged landscape of Japan resulted in a journal that was called *The Narrow Road to the Deep North*. It is a record of events that took place in the year 1689 as Bashō made his way to the northern part of Honshu. Lively descriptions of local inhabitants and a pervasive geography of untamed nature abound. Bashō's reference to himself in his diary as a "beggarly pilgrim" belies his inspiring skills as an astute observer of nearly everything his eye catches sight of, including "a holy tree" on the outskirts of Shirakawa.

IN THE SHADE OF A LARGE CHESTNUT tree near this post town, a Buddhist monk was living a secluded life. It seemed a quiet life, indeed, like that of an ancient poet-recluse who picked horse chestnuts in the depths of the mountains. I wrote down on a piece of paper: "The Chinese ideogram Chestnut consists of two letters that signify West and Tree respectively. Hence Bodhisattva Gyoki is said to have associated a chestnut tree with Western Paradise [the direction of the holy land] and used it both for his cane and for the pillars of his house."[5]

What I know of the divine sciences and Holy Scripture, I learnt in woods and fields. I have had no other masters than the beeches and the oaks.

SAINT BERNARD OF CLAIRVAUX (1091–1153),
BENEDICTINE CONTEMPLATIVE,
VISIONARY, AND EPISTLER[6]

Running Tree

The Reverend Dr. Trusler, an eccentric clergyman, commissioned a drawing from the English poet, artist, and mystic William Blake. Upon seeing it, he took an immediate dislike to it. "*Your Fancy*," he wrote to Blake, ". . . seems to be in the other world, or the World of Spirits, which accords not with my intentions."[7] Undeterred, Blake wrote back (on August 23, 1799) defining the spirit that informed his work: "Imagination or Spiritual Sensation," as he termed it.

THE TREE WHICH MOVES SOME to tears of joy is in the eyes of others only a green thing that stands in the way. Some see nature all ridicule and deformity, and by these I shall not regulate my proportions; and some scarce see nature at all. But to the eyes of the man of imagination, nature is imagination itself. As a man is, so he sees. As the eye is formed, such are its powers. You certainly mistake, when you say that the visions of fancy are not to be found in this world. To me this world is all one continued vision of fancy or imagination. . . .[8]

*A*s a child, George Seferis (1900–1971), Greek poet, essayist, and recipient of the 1963 Nobel Prize in Literature, lived in a world peopled by trees that "smiled" at him and upon him. Trees were his only dreams in childhood. As he began to grow, the trunks of trees played a decisive role in his coming of age. Their roots "tormented" him "when in the warmth of winter they'd come and wind themselves around [his] body." The poet quietly confided: "That's how I got to know my body." Trees introduced Seferis to himself.

The influence of trees persisted. Seferis sought the regenerative powers of his arboreal teachers throughout his adult life.

I KNOW A PINE TREE that leans over near a sea. At mid-day it bestows upon the tired body a shade measured like our life, and in the evening the wind blowing through its needles begins a curious song as though of souls that made an end of death, just at the moment when they begin to become skin and lips again. Once I stayed awake all night under this tree. At dawn I was new, as though I had been freshly quarried.[9]

In the beginning were the waters. Matter readied itself.
The sun glowed. And a lotus slowly opened, holding the
universe on its golden pericarp.

INDIAN CREATION MYTH[10]

*A*s early as 3000 B.C. plants were regarded as "the home of divine spirits with powers beneficial to mankind,"[11] writes Indian author Naveen Patnaik. The renowned sages conducted their dialogues in the forest, he says, "using plants again and again to illustrate concepts of spiritual continuity to their students, because the forest represented the endless self-regeneration of life, or what we would call today an ecosystem, complete in itself."[12] In India plants are honored as sources of enlightenment and metaphors for the ascent of spirit. The lotus, the ideal of symmetry and holiness, symbolizes nonattachment.

TO THE INDIAN IMAGINATION this beautiful water flower is associated with divinity. An early medieval Hindu text describes a goddess as being,

> Slender as a lotus-fiber,
> Lotus-eyed,
> In the lotus posture,
> Pollen dusting her lotus-feet,
> She dwells
> In the pendant lotus of the heart.

More significantly, the lotus is a symbol of enlightenment. Soaring toward the sun, untainted by the clay water in which it grows, the lotus is used by Indian philosophers as an exemplar of the soul— an illustration of the doorway that opens backward into the waters of birth, or forward into revelation.

The lotus is central to the practitioners of *kundalini* yoga, who believe the *kundalini*, or potent occult energy, that lies coiled in man like a sleeping serpent can be awakened through yogic disciplines and meditations. Once aroused, this serpent of wisdom ascends "fine as a lotus-fiber" through a succession of psychic centers described as "lotus-chakras," until it reaches the last and highest chakra, which opens as "the thousand-petaled lotus of understanding," revealing the brightness of the Self like a universal flame no wind has ever disturbed.

Appropriately, the medicinal properties of the lotus appear to aid concentration and Ayurvedic science extracts medicines from the lotus, which are antiallergenic, anti-spasmodic, and astringent. The beauty of the lotus is also considered a medicine.[13]

Ent

*B*rother Lawrence, the seventeenth-century French mystic, relates his first glimpse of God-realization at the age of eighteen upon viewing a tree in which he perceived the tree's creator. His letters, spiritual maxims, and conversations were published after his death in 1691. The "anonymous" recorder of his conversations, M. Beaufort, reports that Brother Lawrence told him:

THAT IN THE WINTER, [UPON] SEEING A TREE stripped of its leaves, and considering that within a little time the leaves would be renewed, and after that the flowers and fruit appear, he received a high view of the Providence and Power of God, which has never since been effaced from his soul. That this view had set him perfectly loose from the world and kindled in him such a love for God that he could not tell whether it had increased in above forty years that he had lived since.[14]

$\mathcal{L}$aurens van der Post (b. 1906), explorer, political adviser, journalist, soldier, farmer, distinguished author, conservationist, and eloquent interpreter of modern South African life, spent his entire childhood amongst the Bushmen, Bantu, and Hottentots of and around his Afrikaans father's farm ("Afrikaans" describes the descendants of seventeenth-century Dutch settlers). "My own story began with the Bushman stories," he recalled in an interview toward the end of his life. "I had a nurse, Klara, who was a Bushman woman, a Stone Age person. Hers was the first human face I can remember. . . . It was one of the dearest faces. Even as I talk about it I am filled with the most incredible emotion."[15] Van der Post's first schooling began with the myths, legends, and stories of his African boyhood friends and his Bushman nurse. "My real education came from stories," he once said. His novels reflect this profound influence out of which he was to be continually reminded that "the master pattern at work within me, the magnet which conditions the field of all my reactions, is African."[16]

In one of his classic works, *A Far-Off Place*, van der Post reveals the depth of impact of his South African roots. Instructions in the ways of the bush and its sacred character, imparted by an elder, are intoned by a young boy as he encounters a pride of seven lions. Compelled to observe the rhythm that serves the law of life in the bush, the old man's words overtake him:

REMEMBER ALWAYS, LITTLE COUSIN, that no matter how awful or insignificant, how ugly or beautiful, it might look to you, everything in the bush has its own right to be there. No one can challenge this right unless compelled by some necessity of life itself. Everything has its own dignity, however absurd it might seem to you, and we are all bound to recognise and respect it as we wish our own to be recognised and respected. Life in the bush is necessity, and it understands all forms of necessity. It will always forgive what is imposed upon it out of necessity, but it will never understand and accept anything less than necessity. And remember that, everywhere, it has its own watchers to see whether the law of necessity is being observed. You may often think that deep in the darkness and the density of the bush you are alone and unobserved, but that, Little Cousin, would be an illusion of the most dangerous kind. One is never alone in the bush. One is never unobserved. One is always known. It is true there are many parts of the bush where no human eye might be able to penetrate but there is always, like some spy of God Himself, an eye upon you, even if it is only the eye of some animal, bird, reptile or little insect, recording in its own way in the book of life how you carry yourself.

And beside the eyes—do not underrate them—there are the tendrils of the plants, the grasses, the leaves of the trees and the roots of all growing things, which lead the warmth of the sun deep down into the darkest and coldest recesses of the earth, to quicken them with new life. They too shake with the shock of our feet and vibrate to the measure of our tread and I am certain have their own ways of registering what we bring or take from the life for which they are a home. Often as I have seen how a blade of grass will suddenly shiver on a windless day at my approach or the leaves of trees tremble, I have thought that they too must have a heart beating within them and that my coming has quickened their pulse with apprehension until I can note the alarm vibrating at their delicate wrists and their high, translucid temples. Often when I have heard a bird suddenly break off its song, some beetle or cricket cease its chanting, because of my presence, I have felt uninvited like an intruder in a concert in some inner chamber of our royal environment and stood reproved for being so rough and not more mindful of my manners.[17]

Walking Stone Guardians

The Chinese landscape painter Shih Lu (1919–1982) was a dissenter who fled to the wilderness in a time of persecution. His image of pines on a sacred mountain in China reflects his admiration for the spirit of Nature and his defiance of tyranny. A poem that accompanied the painting reveals his intimate identification with these arboreal exemplars.

I LOVE THE PINES of Mount Hua,
Tall, noble, solemn, and dignified.
Their thrusting trunks vie with the sun and moon.
Resisting cold winds through the years,
They shake their arms at the sky-scraping ridge
And hold high their heads, like striding blue dragons.
They support the clouds forever,
Without taking flight to the heavens.[18]

*I*mpelled by dreams and visions, ex-soldier and tree activist Allen Meredith has led a one-man crusade across Britain for more than fifteen years to preserve the revered but forgotten and now threatened prehistoric yew. What makes the yew "the immortal tree," says Meredith, is its "power of regeneration [which] would have been obvious thousands of years ago to ancient people." Meredith claims that the yew is "the watcher," the "guardian of the planet"; he has visited the few hundred remaining trees by bicycle, and his solitary, scientific investigations have satisfied leading botanists that the yew is indeed a very ancient tree, quite probably thousands of years old. Meredith is committed to recovering its knowledge and explaining its importance to the vitality of the human spirit.

THE YEW TREE IS THE MOST SACRED thing on this earth, here for some very special reason. If we don't recognize why the yew is here, then I don't think we will survive. What I dreaded was going off this planet without telling people about yew trees: that they are the most important species on earth—including human beings.

The yew tree is part and parcel of each one of us. We evolved from the yew in a sense. It is obviously a divinity; the neolithic people would have seen that. Generation after generation has seen these things living on; that is why the ancient yew tree is so important.[19]

In 1913 Rabindranath Tagore (1861–1941) became the first Asian to receive the Nobel Prize in Literature. Born in Calcutta the fourteenth child of a wealthy Bengali family, Tagore composed approximately one hundred books of verse including the renowned *Gitanjali* ("Song Offerings")—103 short poems on the love of God—50 dramas, and numerous novels, short stories, and essays. He was also a world traveler, painter, composer, actor, commentator on international affairs, and great spiritual presence. In 1915 he was knighted but repudiated the title after a massacre by British troops in Amritsar in 1919. Tagore believed in the fundamental unity of all great spiritual truths and once wrote, "the great Ganges must not hesitate to declare its essential similarity to the Nile of Egypt, or to the Yangtse-Kiang of China."[20] He spent his life closely observing the human experience and its relation to the divine, an exploration that began at an early age in his own backyard.

WE HAD A SMALL GARDEN beside our house; it was a fairyland to me, where miracles of beauty were of everyday occurrence. Every morning at an early hour I would run out from my bed to greet the first pink flush of dawn through the trembling leaves of the coconut trees which stood in a line along the garden boundary. The dewdrops glistened as the grass caught the first tremor of the morning breeze. The sky seemed to bring a personal companionship, and my whole body drank in the light and peace of those silent hours. I was anxious never to miss a single morning, because each one was more precious to me than gold to the miser.

I had been blessed with that sense of wonder which gives a child his right to enter the treasure-house of mystery in the heart of existence. I neglected my studies because they took me from my friend and companion, the world around me; and when I was thirteen I freed myself from the clutches of an educational system that tried to imprison me with lessons.

Perhaps this will explain the meaning of my religion. The world was alive, intimately close to my life. I still remember my repulsion when a medical student brought me a piece of human windpipe and tried to excite my admiration for its structure. He tried to convince me that it was the source of the beautiful human voice, but I rejected that information with disgust. I did not admire the skill of the workman, but rather the artist who concealed the machinery and revealed his unified creation.[21]

Tree Spirit

He is out of sight, but I put my ear to a tree in the forest, and that brings me the sound, and I hear when the moose makes his next leap and I follow. . . . I follow always, listening now and then with my ear against a tree.

BEDAGI (BIG THUNDER), WABANAKI, CA. 1907[22]

*K*nown to her contemporaries as "the Sibyl of the Rhine," the twelfth-century seer Hildegard of Bingen—founder and first abbess of the Benedictine Rhineland community at Bingen—led a fascinating and extraordinarily active life until her death at the age of eighty-one. Born into German aristocracy and raised in a nunnery, Hildegard's writing achievements alone—apart from her musicianship and painting—are remarkable particularly given the fact that she did not set pen to paper until her forty-third year. They included a colossal trilogy covering ethics, cosmology, and church doctrine, two scientific works of an encyclopedic nature about medicine and natural science, hundreds of letters to people in all walks of life, the biographies of two saints, seventy liturgical songs, and the first known morality play.[23]

The *Scivias* (short for *Scito vias Domini* or "Know the Ways of the Lord") was the first of Hildegard's visionary labors. Written and recorded over a ten-year period (1141–51), the manuscript received the approval of Pope Eugenius III granting Hildegard and her work immediate recognition. The *Scivias* today is considered an important medieval summa. It comprises twenty-six visions divided into three "books" offering innumerable perspectives on Christian doctrine and exploring such diverse themes as the nature of heaven and earth, the sacraments, tenets of the moral life, and the relation between microcosm and macrocosm. The earliest surviving manuscript (1165) is illuminated with thirty-five impressive miniatures accompanied by lyrics and a short play. The following description of the nature of the soul is from Book One.

THE SOUL IN THE BODY is like sap in a tree, and the soul's powers are like the form of the tree. How? The intellect in the soul is like the greenery of the tree's branches and leaves, the will like its flowers, the mind like its bursting firstfruits, the reason like the perfected mature fruit, and the senses like its size and shape. And so a person's body is strengthened and sustained by the soul. Hence, O human, understand what you are in your soul. . . .[24]

Old Man of the Hoh

It was said of an old man that he dwelt in Syria on the way to the desert. This was his work: whenever a monk came from the desert he gave him refreshment with all his heart. Now one day an anchorite came, to whom he gave refreshment, but the other did not want to accept it, saying he was fasting. Filled with sorrow, the old man said to him, "Do not disregard your servant, I beg you; do not despise me, but let us pray. Look at the tree which is here—we will follow the way of whichever of us causes it to bend when he kneels on the ground and prays." So the anchorite knelt down to pray, and nothing happened. Then the hospitable one knelt down, and at once the tree bent towards him. Taught by this, they gave thanks to God.

THE WISDOM OF THE DESERT FATHERS[25]

*I*n his autobiographical account of his people, the Stoneys, who are native to the Saskatchewan River country in what is now known as southern Alberta in Canada, Chief John Snow's grandfather, Walking Buffalo, suggests that a person must seek to emulate his arboreal brothers and sisters.

MY GRANDFATHER . . . TOLD ME one day that I must look at the beautiful forest where the trees and shrubs and tiny plants grow in a harmony of variety. He pointed out to me how some trees grow tall and straight to shelter the small trees and the misshapen ones; how the delicate flowers nestle among the grass at the foot of the trees catching the sunlight, as though the trees lean away to allow its rays to give them life. He spoke of the red trees and the white trees and the black trees, each forming a part of a beautiful pattern in their diversity. He showed me how each stands proud and upright in its own way to honour the Maker, the Great Spirit. The diversity of plants and trees makes a beautiful forest. Why is the forest beautiful? Because it grows according to the plan of the Creator. If mankind too could stand humbly at the Creator's feet, mankind too could share in the harmony which is the Creation.[26]

In the winter of 1680, a stock of basho tree (a certain species of banana tree) was presented to Matsuo Bashō (1644–1694), haiku poet and pilgrim, by one of his disciples. Bashō developed an immediate and special attachment to this species of tree. His residence came to be known as the Bashō ("banana plant"), and Master Bashō, shortly thereafter, accepted his new name and used it for the rest of his life. He leaves us in no doubt about his feelings for this arboreal friend and companion spirit.

THE LEAVES OF THE BASHO tree are large enough to cover a harp. When they are wind-broken, they remind me of the injured tail of a phoenix, and when they are torn, they remind me of a green fan ripped by the wind. The tree does bear flowers, but unlike other flowers, there is nothing gay about them. The big trunk of the tree is untouched by the axe, for it is utterly useless as building wood. I love the tree, however, for its very uselessness . . . I sit underneath it, and enjoy the wind and rain that blow against it.[27]

Tree Awakening

We have seen, you and I, the laughing sirens of the trees.
We have been fortunate because, it is said, they are rarely
seen, if ever, that they never venture beyond the forest of
pine and cedar but stay in the shadows of the thicket of
the wood. It is said that these women you have seen cannot think for themselves, that their minds are not their
own. It is said that the women you have seen before your
eyes go through life with no intent but to frolic, to make
merry and to laugh. It is said that the young who fall and
are seduced into their camp return not unto their own but
stay with the creatures who think not and cannot reason
to know what is good and what is evil. It is said that if in
your ramblings you hear this laughter in the wood behind
a tree, tarry not, but turn and go the other way. It is said
that this is difficult to do when one is young.

"Laughter Behind the Trees" from the
Tloo-qwah-nah ceremony, told by
George Clutesi, Nootka writer and artist[28]

When her family moved to an Oregon logging community at the turn of the century, Opal Whitely (b. 1897) kept a diary from the age of six until she was nine of her new home—the forest and its ways. The diary was published in 1920 and caused an uproar. *The Story of Opal: The Story of an Understanding Heart* was called a fraud for it was thought that no little girl could have written it. In the following passage from her childhood memories, Opal writes out of a translucent intimacy with her true origins.

I SO DO LOVES TREES. I have thinks I was once a tree, growing in the forest. Now all trees are my brothers. . . .

Most every day, I do dance. I dance with the leaves and the grass. I feel thrills from my toes to my curls. I feel like a bird, sometimes. Then I spread my arms for wings, and I go my way from stump to stump, on adown the hill. Sometimes I am a demoiselle, flitting near unto the water. Then I nod unto the willows, and they nod unto me. They wave their arms, and I wave mine. They wiggle their toes in the water a bit, and I do so, too. And every time we wiggle our toes, we do drink into our souls the song of the brook—the glad song it is always singing. And the joy-song does sing on in our hearts. So did it today.[29]

The Buddhist scriptures tell us there are eight objections to living in a house: it is a lot of trouble to build; it must be kept in repair; some nobleman might seize it; too many people may want to live in or visit it; it makes the body tender; it provides concealment for committing evil deeds; it causes pride of ownership; and it harbors lice and bugs.

There are ten advantages, on the other hand, in residing under a tree: it can be found with ease; it can be found in any locality; the sight of falling leaves is a reminder of the impermanence of life; a tree arouses no covetous thoughts; it affords no opportunity for evil deeds; it is not received from any person; it is inhabited by good spirits; it needs no fence; it promotes health; it does not involve worldly attachments.

PUJIMALIYA, INDIAN SAGE; A PALI CANON

*I*n his novel *Comes the Voyager at Last*, a journey of mythic consciousness through the mental landscape of his African world, Kofi Awoonor, Ghanaian poet, novelist, teacher, and diplomat, attests to the symbolic, creative, and unitive power of the natural landscape and its imprint upon "the most fundamental framework of our existence."

In Awoonor's mythic forest, trees are cathedrals of the spirit. They are portals to ascension and re-memberment.

NIGHT WAS UPON US when we entered the forest only to be assailed by a thick impenetrable darkness thickened by tall trees whose canopies covered our skies and the eyes of the heavens. Beneath our weary feet was a soft carpet of rotting leaves. A magic smell of mould and decay rose everywhere.

We camped near the first giant tree for the night. The night was a whining long moan of trees as they whispered in the periodic winds that rushed through the few lingering patches of cleared ground. We managed a few fitful winks of sleep punctuated by neighborly nightmares of screams and wild speech. It has been the same every night of our journey. . . .

The giant trees reached almost to the heavens. Tall, erect their bases were large ominous temples of marching feet that supported shrines and homes of gods and spirits. From the heavens their crowns dropped occasional dew and twigs. Several climbers clung upon their bodies like beads on the devotees of a god. Lichens and epiphytes were the thoroughfare of squirrels and the mouse-faced woodpecker that flit from under tree to under tree. The sacred Logo tree stood guard over the forest at legendary intervals humming with all the supervisory deities long known chants of ancient rites. Birdsong and dirge for the dead days of our lives everywhere, life above and around, beneath, putrefaction, decay to nurture life and the tree. The trees would swoon now with a solemnity that was the signal of distress in their heavens high above our sorrow. It seemed they have been called upon by their very nature to share and hearken unto our inner sorrows swaying, in giddy waves in a melancholy jubilee in the heart of the forest and our souls.[30]

Green Man

You are the forest.

You are all the great trees.

O Lord White As Jasmine,

filling and filled by all.

Why don't you show me your face?

MAHADEVIYAKKA,

HYMN TO SIVA (TWELFTH CENTURY A.D.)[31]

I went to the woods because I wished to live deliberately, to front only the essential facts of life, and see if I could learn what it had to teach, and not, when I come to die, discover that I had not lived," wrote Henry David Thoreau in his quest for a simple and good life and the "higher laws" of existence. In a passage from his essay "Walking," he glimpses some of these spiritual realities.

WHEN I WOULD RECREATE MYSELF, I seek the darkest wood, the thickest and most interminable and, to the citizen, most dismal swamp. I enter a swamp as a sacred place,—a *sanctum sanctorum*. There is the strength, the marrow of Nature. The wild-wood covers the virgin mould,—and the same soil is good for men and trees.[32]

Torso

I think of earth as the floor of a cathedral where altar and Presence are everywhere," wrote the Irish agriculturalist, painter, poet, and mystic George William Russell. "This reverence came to me as a boy listening to the voice of birds one coloured evening in summer, when suddenly birds and trees and grass and tinted air and myself seemed but one mood or companionship, and I felt a certitude that the same spirit was in all."[33] From the green hills and "the place of rocks" in the countryside surrounding Dublin, the poet was introduced to the numinous nature of Earth itself, the ultimate sacred place:

[W]HEN I LAY ON THE HILL OF KILMASHEOGUE . . . Earth revealed itself to me as a living being, and rock and clay were made transparent so that I saw lovelier and lordlier beings than I had known before, and was made partner in memory of mighty things, happenings in ages long sunken behind time. . . .

[T]he earth is not at all what the geographers suppose it to be . . . Sometimes lying on the hillside with the eyes of the body shut as in sleep I could see valleys and hills, lustrous as a jewel, where all was self-shining, the colours brighter and purer, yet making a softer harmony together than the colours of the world I know. The winds sparkled as they blew hither and thither, yet far distances were clear through that glowing air. What was far off was precise as what was near, and the will to see hurried me to what I desired. There, too, in that land I saw fountains as of luminous mist jetting from some hidden heart of power, and shining folk who passed into those fountains inhaled them and drew life from the magical air. There were, I believe, those who in the ancient world gave birth to legends of nymph and dryad. Their perfectness was like the perfectness of a flower, a beauty which had never, it seemed, been broken by act of the individualised will which with us makes possible a choice between good and evil, and the marring of the mould of natural beauty. . . . [T]hese were my first visions of supernature.[34]

George Nakashima (b. 1905), world-renowned Japanese woodworker, believes that each mature tree is a divine body, "a god consciousness." He has spent his life in the presence of trees. His kinship with trees began with the great forest giants of Washington State's Ho River valley when as a boy he roamed the rain forests of the Olympic Mountains. Later, in Japan, he encountered the twelve-hundred-year-old *keyaki*, an oriental elm, which heightened his sense of wonder and "spurred [him] in [his] search for the origin of the noble tree." The marvel, he has come to understand, is in their being. The personal relationships he has cherished has been with "these awesome cathedrals of the forest."

A TREE PROVIDES PERHAPS OUR MOST INTIMATE contact with nature. A tree sits like an avatar, an embodiment of the immutable, far beyond the pains of man. There are specimens, like the Yaku *sugi*, a type of Japanese cedar, which in their single lives have spanned the entire history of civilized man. These specimens were already substantial trees when Mohenjo-Daro [the Indus Valley civilization, ca. 2500–1900 B.C., located in the transborder area between modern India and Pakistan] was in flower and Europe lived in caves. Hundreds of generations have marched past. Civilizations much greater than ours have risen and turned to dust.

We woodworkers have the audacity to shape timber from these noble trees. In a sense it is our Karma Yoga, the path of action we must take to lead to our union with the Divine. Each tree, each part of each tree, has its own particular destiny and its own special relationship to be fulfilled. We roam the world to find our relationships with these trees.

There was a cedar from the Island of Yaku [off the south coast of Japan's southernmost major island, Kyushu] with a rotted-out core as large as a small cottage. Hundreds of years before it had been cut down for timber, some thirty feet above ground level. Now, its remains stood, surrounded by a crown of small trees which sprang from its living cambium, or outside layer. . . .

We work with boards from these trees, to fulfill their yearning for a second life, to release their richness and beauty. From these planks we fashion objects useful to man, and if nature wills, things of beauty. In any case, these objects harmonize the rhythms of nature to fulfill the tree's destiny and ours. . . . [E]very piece of wood is awesome for it contains the majesty of all the divine forces that exist on the plane of nature's own objects. . . .

We are left in awe by the nobility of a tree, its eternal patience, its suffering caused by man and sometimes nature, its witness to thousands of years of earth's history, its creations of fabulous beauty. It does nothing but good, with its prodigious ability to serve, it gives off its bounty of oxygen while absorbing gases harmful to other living things. The tree and its pith [first material to sprout from a seed] live on. Its fruits feed us. Its branches shade and protect us. And, finally, when time and weather bring it down, its body offers timber for our houses and boards for our furniture. The tree lives on.[35]

Embracing Roots

Worldly people lose the roots and cling to the tree-tops.

AN ANCIENT ADEPT'S DESCRIPTION
OF SPIRITUAL AMNESIA[36]

Breathing in, breathing out. Slow deep inhale, slow deep exhale. Quieting the body, quieting the mind. I woke up this morning under the graceful, arching branches of bay laurels and Douglas firs. All night the trees have been conversing under the full moon, weaving me into their stories, capturing my dreams with their leaning limbs and generous trunks. Breathing together as I slept, as they rested, we danced quietly in the summer night. Their great confidence framed a circle for my waking; their sturdy presence offered an invitation to be still.

STEPHANIE KAZA, AUTHOR, NATURALIST,
AND MEDITATOR IN THE ZEN PRACTICE
OF *SHIKANTAZA*—JUST SITTING[37]

Redwood Sage

*S*cholar and environmentalist Stephanie Kaza calls the redwoods "the yogis of the forest," alluding to the trees' transcendent and serene presence. "My journey," writes Kaza in her moving volume of meditations, "conversations" (as she calls them) with her giant exemplars, "is a search for the depths of truth held by these magnificent trees."[38]

FORTUNATELY THE GIANT REDWOODS have not been claimed by any single spiritual tradition as a sacred site. The temples are accessible to visitors from all religious and nonreligious backgrounds; anyone may come and experience awe and humility in these groves. Most of the well-known sites are held in the public trust, protecting the opportunity to pay respect to living beings older and far more enduring than oneself. Offering homage to the trees, one cultivates ecological virtue, gaining some sense of the evolutionary miracle that spawned human life.

The North Grove at Calaveras is one of seventy-five temples in a 250-mile section of the Sierra Nevada. The trees grow primarily in groves rather than as isolated individuals, preferring moist sites at 5,000 to 7,000 feet on the western slope. The relative rarity of the groves, existing as relict populations from an earlier, wider distribution, adds to the sense of encounter with the unusual. Today's sequoias are limited at higher elevations by harsh winters and at lower elevations by lack of water.

One could compare these groves to the ancient temples of Athens, or Machu Picchu, or Stonehenge. But the redwood trees are not ruins, they are still alive. Each grove is part of an unbroken gene flow originating millions of years ago. Each mature tree is a living history over 2,000 years old. These are very old churches. But the sequoias do not look old or ruined; they radiate a dynamic vitality that dwarfs all other trees in the area.

A visitor to these sacred groves might be lured into believing that sequoias are always still and undisturbed. But there is a secret here. The true nature of these trees is intimately related to fire, element of spirit. The fibrous, thick bark wraps the tree in a fireproof robe; yet the seeds depend on fire to germinate. Without fire to clear the ground, the trees do not regenerate. . . . In the life of a sequoia, decades might go by with no new seedlings. But then, suddenly—fire races through the grove, leaping and burning. . . .

A pilgrimage to the Big Trees is a chance to remember the capacity to burn with the fire of existence. Seeing this, one can recognize the same capacity within oneself for new life reborn of passion, for clearing that brings renewal. The blessing of the pilgrim is the journey itself. To align one's journey with the power of trees is to reach beyond the ordinary to the temples of truth.[39]

Behold the herbs! Their virtues are invisible and yet they can be detected.

PARACELSUS (1493–1541),
PHYSICIAN, NATURAL PHILOSOPHER,
ALCHEMIST, AND MYSTIC[40]

*I*ndia's most ancient and esteemed body of wisdom lies in the hymns of the Vedas, the revealed scriptures of the Hindus. Considered to be eternal truths, they are the cornerstone of Hinduism and have been described as "a unique document of the religious consciousness of all humanity."[41] The four Vedas—the *Rig*, the *Sama*, the *Yajur,* and the *Atharva*—together contain more than a hundred thousand verses that range in subject matter from prayers for progeny and prosperity to hymns revering the divine powers of the natural world along with a fascinating array of medical prescriptions. The *Rig* Veda, for example, espouses the concept of humankind as a single family and the essential unity of all spiritual paths. Some of the hymns in the *Rig* honor the powers and grace of the plant world such as the "Hymn in Praise of Herbs," circa 2500 B.C.:

> You herbs, born at the birth of time,
> More ancient than the gods themselves.
> O Plants, with this hymn I sing to you
> Our mothers and our gods.
>
> The holy fig tree is your home.
> A thousand are your growths.
> You, who have a thousand powers,
> Free this my patient from disease.
>
> Fly, Spirit of Disease.
> Be gone with the bluejay and the kingfisher.
> Fly with the wind's impetuous speed.
> Vanish together with the storm.

Most excellent of all are you, O·Plants.
Your vassals are the trees.
Let him be subject to your powers
The man who seeks to injure You.

When restoring vanished strength
I hold you herbs within my hand.
And the Spirit of Disease departs,
Cheated of another death.

Reliever is your mother's name.
Hence, restorers are you called.
Rivers are you, with wings that fly.
Keep distant that which brings disease.

Unharmed be he who digs you up.
Unharmed the man for whom I dig.
And let no malady destroy
The lives within your guardianship.[42]

In the great Javanese epic poem the *Ardjuna Wiwaha* ("Celebrations of Ardjuna's Wedding"), inspired by the Mahabharata and composed by Mpu Kanwa in A.D. 1035, seven heavenly nymphs are sent to test Ardjuna's steadfastness. As they approach the grotto on Mount Indrakila where Ardjuna sits deep in meditation, they are treated to an arboreal paradise.

IT WAS MORNING WHEN THEY ARRIVED THERE, and playfully they proceeded on foot along the path. The *tjamara* [pine-like] trees swayed on the slopes [as if] extending courteous greetings at the sight of the nymphs. The cinnamon trees, whose [glowing red] young leaves palpitated daintily, seemed to call out audibly, rivaling in loveliness and redness the nymphs' breasts and lips. The shapes of the beguiling trees of the forests were hidden in clouds, however; it was misty, one could hardly see; only that which was nearby was visible; as one moved away it was closed in again by mist. The yellow *sekara* [palm blossom] trees had just grown young leaves; one tried to see the bees which hummed but remained invisible. Peacocks preened themselves, spreading their wings, standing opposite each other on the dead trunk of a *tjandana* [sandalwood] tree.[43]

Pachyderm

In the spirit of Marcel Proust's *Remembrance of Things Past,* in which his character uses the taste and aroma of a madeleine to trigger memories, Regina O'Melveny's ginkgo tree has a comparable effect. The tree "that predates the dinosaurs and first appeared in great swampy forests" is a symbol of happier times for O'Melveny. It evokes for her a childhood idyll.

WHEN I WAS BORN, thirty-nine years ago, my parents planted a ginkgo tree in my honor. . . . I have no idea why my parents chose this tree, and since I can no longer ask them, I imagine that my mother loved the delicate fans of ginkgo leaves as they trembled with tenderness in the spring. My father may have loved the Oriental elegance of the tree which he painted with *sumi* inks. Their love for me was the tree.

The ginkgo with its knobby joints and long shoots sat in a stout pot on the uneven bricks of the patio. A hot Santa Ana wind blasted the tree until its yellow leaves fluttered wildly and tore loose, spinning all over the patio, crowding the steps, and flattening against the door and windows. The late October light made the leaves shimmer as they careened and plummeted. The ginkgo was the only deciduous tree in our Southern California back yard, so the miracle of leaves which turned golden and then were swept up in the light astonished me. It was as if a Mandarin book of golden pages had split its binding and bits of precious paper flew all around me. My mother had been reading Chinese and Japanese fairy tales to me, and now I found myself in the middle of one, a tale which had begun to unfold at my birth. I began to collect the leaves for my dolls. They were unlike any leaves I had ever seen. The fine veins spread from the stem like the spokes of my bicycle wheels. I could put four of the softly curved triangles together to make a full circle, or two for a bow or butterfly wings. By themselves, the leaves were perfect fans for the Japanese porcelain doll, draped in a red and blue kimono. I placed ginkgo fans near her feet clad in wooden sandals, or tried to fit leaves into her white hands sewn to the front of her kimono.

I can't quite recall when the ginkgo died, but I know it was before we moved, when I was thirteen. Our family was falling apart and many things fell through the cracks, including my dolls, which my mother summarily bagged and sent to Goodwill.

The next time I saw a ginkgo tree, twenty years later, I was visiting New York for the first time and was amazed to see whole streets lined with ginkgo trees. Somehow I never expected to see another ginkgo, and yet here avenues of ginkgoes opened before me, a green corridor of light, doors flung open to reveal an expanse of ancient forest. A wild and deeply rooted hope clenched my heart. I picked up a leaf and slid it between the pages of my journal.[44]

Almost all the Hindus . . . adore a plant like our *Basilico gentile*, but of more pungent odor. Every one before his house has a little altar . . . in the middle of which they erect certain pedestals like little towers, and in these the shrub is grown.

P. VINCENZO MARIA, A VOYAGE TO INDIA (1672)[45]

aveen Patnaik, author and founding member of the Indian National Trust for Art and Cultural Heritage, has a special interest in the healing plants of India. In *The Garden of Life* he explicates the genesis of the *Ayurveda*, traditional Indian medical science or the "Knowledge of Life," whose foundation, he says, rests upon India's ancient veneration of plants and their medicinal properties. Holy basil is but one example of nature's beneficence held in sacred trust not only by the Ayurvedic physician but also by many others in the Indian lay population.

MODERN SCIENCE HAS ESTABLISHED that this modest aromatic shrub perceptibly purifies the air within a wide radius of its vicinity, proving most effective just before sunrise, the time when it is ritually circled by the devout.

Perhaps this is why Hindu myths say the King of Death himself gives way before this holy shrub, and why each year, at the waxing of the autumn moon, the plant is married in a religious ritual to one of the three gods of the Hindu trinity, Vishnu the Preserver.

Any domestic courtyard which is centered around the holy basil is considered in India a place of peace, piety, and virtue.

The plant's roots symbolize religious pilgrimage, its branches divinity, its crown an understanding of the scriptures. Traditionally, once the shrub has been planted in an Indian courtyard it is nurtured for three months before it is worshipped with offerings of rice, flowers, and lighted lamps. After that, virgins pray to the holy basil for husbands, married women for domestic peace and prosperity.

Medically, the plant provides a pharmacopoeia for the entire household. Its leaves are crushed in honey and used to cure coughs, colds, and bronchitis, and to reduce fevers. An infusion of basil leaves and ginger is India's most popular remedy for stomachaches in children. Its essential oil is an antiseptic and insect repellent, while its root, reduced to paste, soothes bites and stings, acting even as an antidote to snake venom and scorpion bites.[46]

Ecstatic Tree

There rose a tree. O magic transcendence!
Orpheus sings! And in the ear a tree!

RAINER MARIA RILKE (1875–1926), *SONNETS TO ORPHEUS*[47]

I shall enchant my heart, and I shall place it upon the top
of the flower of the cedar.

EGYPTIAN D'ORSIGNY PAPYRUS[48]

*I*n her superb collection of Haitian folktales, *The Magic Orange Tree*, storyteller and mythologist Diane Wolkstein introduces us to "the strange fruit of the Haitian night" and invites us to suspend our own worlds as the drum announces the entrance of the spirits and the moment of the entrancing realm of story commences. The will to live is at the heart of the song and story (*contes chantés*) of the titular magic orange tree. A corollary to that, observes Wolkstein, is that trees are believed to be a precious communal yardstick: they provide a symbolic measure of life for most everyone.

WHEN A CHILD IS BORN in the countryside, the umbilical cord may be saved and dried and planted in the earth, with a pit from a fruit tree placed on top of the cord. The tree that grows then belongs to the child. And when the tree gives fruit in five or six years, that fruit is considered the property of the child, who can barter or sell it. (Young children in Haiti very quickly become economically active.) Trees in Haiti are thus thought to protect children and are sometimes referred to as the guardian angel of the child. However, if the tree should die or grow in a deformed manner, that would be considered an evil omen for the child who owned the tree.[49]

"Adam and Eve"

$\mathcal{W}$riting in the third person, poet Rainer Maria Rilke (1875–1926) describes a cosmic experience he had in the garden at Duino, near Trieste, in 1912 while resting against the forking of two branches of a tree.

GRADUALLY HIS ATTENTION WAS AWAKENED by a hitherto unknown sensation: it was as if almost imperceptible vibrations were passing from the interior of the tree into him. . . .[H]e was more and more surprised, indeed impressed, by the effect produced in himself by what was passing over into him without ceasing: he felt he had never been filled with more delicate vibrations, his body was being treated in some sort like a soul. . . .[H]e could not, in the first moments, properly distinguish which sense it was by which he was receiving so delicate and pervading a communication; furthermore, the condition it was producing within him was so perfect and so persistent, different from all others, but so little to be represented by the heightening of anything he had ever experienced, that, for all its delicious quality, he could not think of calling it pleasure. . . .[H]e insistently asked himself what was happening to him and almost immediately found an expression which satisfied him, as he said aloud to himself that he had reached the other side of Nature. . . .[H]is body became indescribably touching to him and of no other use than that he might be present in it, purely and cautiously, exactly like a ghost. . . . Looking round him slowly, without otherwise altering his position, he recognized everything, remembered it, smiled at it as it were with distant affection. . . . He looked at a passing bird, a shadow attracted his attention, even the path itself, the way it went on and passed out of sight, filled him with thoughtful insight. . . . A periwinkle standing near, whose blue gaze he had often already seen, came to him now from a more spiritual distance, but with such inexhaustible significance, as if nothing more were now to be concealed. Altogether he became aware that all objects appeared to him now more distant and at the same time, somehow or other, more true.

Saying to himself from time to time that this could not last, he yet did not fear the cessation of this extraordinary condition, as if only such an ending could be expected of it as was, like that of music, in complete conformity with law.[50]

The late Forrest Carter's skillful use of language in his beguiling and controversial autobiography, The Education of Little Tree, *brings the rhythms of hill talk alive in a way that sings Little Tree's adventures into a memorable and universal experience. In what follows, Little Tree shares his Cherokee maternal grandfather's "tree-thought."*

GRANMA'S PA WAS CALLED Brown Hawk. She said his understanding was deep. He could feel the tree-thought. Once, she said, when she was a little girl, her Pa was troubled and said the white oaks on the mountain was excited and scared. He spent much time on the mountain, walking among the oaks. They were of much beauty, tall and straight. They wasn't selfish, allowing ground for sumach and persimmon, and hickory and chestnut to feed the wild things. Not being selfish gave them much spirit and the spirit was strong.

Granma said her Pa got so worried about the oaks that he would walk amongst them at night, for he knew something was wrong.

Then, early one morning, as the sun broke the mountain ridge, Brown Hawk watched while lumbermen moved through the white oaks, marking and figuring how to cut all of them down. When they left, Brown Hawk said, the white oaks commenced to cry. And he could not sleep. So he watched the lumbermen. They built a road up to the mountain over which to bring their wagons.

Granma said her Pa talked to the Cherokees and they determined to save the white oaks. She said at night, when the lumbermen would leave and go back to the settlement, the Cherokees would dig up the road, hacking deep trenches across it. The women and children helped. . . .

Granma said it was a hard struggle and they grew tired. Then one day, as the lumbermen were working on the road, a giant white oak fell across a wagon. It killed two mules and smashed the wagon. She said it was a fine, healthy white oak and had no reason to fall, but it did.

The lumbermen gave up trying to build the road. Spring rains set in . . . and they never came back.

Granma said the moon waxed full, and they held a celebration in the great stand of white oaks. They danced in the full yellow moon, and the white oaks sang and touched their branches together, and touched the Cherokee. Granma said they sang a death chant for the white oak who had given his life to save others, and she said the feeling was so strong that it almost picked her up off the mountain.

"Little Tree," she said, "these things you must not tell, for it will not help to tell them in this world that is the white man's. But you must know. And so I have told you."[51]

Tree Hands

Be still, my heart, these great trees are prayers.

RABINDRANATH TAGORE, BENGALI POET,

ESSAYIST, COMPOSER, AND MYSTIC[52]

Reaching up to Heaven the Lotus leaves melt into an
infinity of green.

SU TUNG-P'O (SUNG DYNASTY, A.D. 960–1276),

POET, PAINTER, ESSAYIST, HUMORIST, AND CALLIGRAPHIST[53]

Among trees I am the Asvattha.

KRISHNA, *THE BHAGAVAD GITA* (200 B.C.–A.D. 200)[54]

*ndian author Naveen Patnaik explores the holy myths of the sacred fig tree. There are two species of Indian fig—the asvattha and the banyan—both of which have been described as the Tree of Enlightenment. Patnaik ascribes to the asvattha the symbolic qualities of the Cosmic Tree or Eternal Tree. Other views, however, attribute a comparable sacredness to the banyan.

LORD KRISHNA'S METAPHOR in the holy book of the Hindus is easily understood by Indians who believe the wood of the *Asvattha* or sacred fig was used to light the original sacred fire with which the gods granted knowledge to the human race.

India honors the sacred fig as the Tree of Life. The earliest evidence of this reverence was discovered by archaeologists excavating the five-thousand-year-old remains of the Indus Valley civilization, when they found seals already depicting the sacred fig circled by worshippers. Today, believers still sit under the sacred fig, meditating on the Creator.

In ancient India the constant whisper of leaves on the sacred fig's elongated leaf stems was likened to the hum of India's oldest musical instrument, the vina or lute, and the planting of fig trees was both an act of merit and a means of ratifying peace treaties. As befits the tree of life, its medical properties were found to contribute to the health of the vital functions—circulation, vision, the lungs, and the kidneys.

So deeply is this tree associated with both the origin and the symbiosis of life that it is thought to induce illumination, and countless Indian legends tell of sages meditating in its shade. The greatest of them came to be known as Enlightened One or the Buddha, and his tree the Bodhi, or Tree of Enlightenment. Buddhists often depict the Buddha in the shape of this tree, which has become the Buddhist symbol of consciousness.

In 288 B.C. the Indian emperor Asoka gifted a graft of the tree under which the Buddha had meditated, to the king of Sri Lanka. Today that grafted tree is still circled by chanting devotees.

When the original boddhi tree withered in India, a graft from the Sri Lankan tree was planted in its place, where it continues to provide a living link between the Buddha and those who seek enlightenment.[55]

Feline Spirit

Here, my brothers, are the roots of trees, here are empty places; meditate.

Ancient Buddhist philosopher[56]

*I*n his first novel *Wales' Work*, Canadian writer Robert Walshe delivers a wild account of a dead publisher's last wishes perceived from the point of view of a corpse incarnate. It is a metaphysical adventure, a psychic shake-out, that makes you wonder about who is really dead or living. Nineteen envelopes contain the deceased protagonist's instructions about the dispersal of his bodily and worldly remains and the philosophy that goes along with them. Nothing is what it seems. A great bag of tricks that is interspersed throughout a series of requests left by Wales conspires to reveal an unknown Wales and alter the thinking of some of those he left behind. A contemplative Wales, for example, discloses an "uncharacteristic" affinity for a garden that flourished by his former upside-down house in Kent, built into a hillside next to a field of Saskatchewan wheatcorn.

I MUST TELL YOU ONE DAY what those trees came to mean to me—particularly the birches, and the mountain ash with its flashes of scarlet colour memorializing my native land. As it took root and pushed out its first timid foliage I began to see it and the wheatfield above, far more than any passport or dull entry in a statistician's ledger, as my totems of place. I planted the tree as a way of leaving something living behind me. Trees are not eternal stone, but they remind us that stone had once been living fire, and sometimes served, while it cooled, as flowerpress, seedbed, agaragar for petrifying fish. Just as stone will outlast us, our trees, too, will outlive the fragile traces we make such a show of leaving in our names. Meanwhile the leaves may bud and flourish and sear and fall, and birds may find a home in their branches. Every man who is not a carver of stone should plant a tree and nourish it, when the day comes, with the remnants of his bones.[57]

A yew is just as important as Durham Cathedral, and a hell of a sight older.

DAVID BELLAMY,
BRITISH BOTANIST AND CONSERVATIONIST[58]

$\mathcal{S}$ir George Trevelyan enjoins us to awaken to the unique spiritual significance of a magnificent tree, the incomparable yew.

WHAT MAGIC IS THERE IN THE ANCIENT YEW TREES! What is it in them that fires our vision and fills the soul with mystery, touching ageless history?

We associate our yew trees with our churchyards. There we constantly find them gracing the church and spreading their great arms among the graves. And many people may tacitly assume that the "old folk" planted yews in churchyards. But no! The great yew trees can be 2,000 years old, or 3,000, or, in some cases, they may reach 4,000 years or more, and our churches were mostly built less than 1,000 years ago. The yews came first, planted on sacred sites known to the Druids. The later church builders were sensitive to the holy places and knew where to build their churches. So let us awaken to the wonder of the yews, planted long before the churches were built, and linked with ancient pre-Christian ritual and mystery.

What a marvel is the ancient yew! It is claimed that the great yew could be absolutely immortal. Grasp what it is doing. The central complex of bole and trunk often seems like a number of trees flowing into each other to make an entity of incredible strength. Then the branches around the central trunk dip down and reroot themselves so that, as a virtually new tree, they may send out further branches. Thus, theoretically at least, the process can go on till the ringed complex covers a great area.

Our imagination is fired by this tree. Once we have "seen" a yew tree, then it becomes fascinating to study the complex bole and see how the streams of energy flow along its ribs. Our imaginative vision can merge with the wondrous structure. Theoretically, the yew tree could be ageless and never die, the central trunk like a compact pillar of immense strength.[59]

There is in India a tree whose property it is to plant itself.
It spreads out mighty arms to the earth, where in the
space of a single year the arms take root and put forth
anew.

PLINY (A.D. 70), ON THE WONDROUS BANYAN TREE
(SANSKRIT NAME: *NYAGRODHA*; HINDI NAME: *BAR*)[60]

Baucis and Philemon

The leaves of the tree are for the healing of the nations.

REVELATION 22:2

Its lands are high [with] very lofty mountains. . . . All are most beautiful . . . and all are accessible and filled with trees of a thousand kinds and tall, and they seem to touch the sky. And I am told that they never lose their foliage . . . and some of them were flowering, some bearing fruit, and some in another stage, according to their nature.

CHRISTOPHER COLUMBUS[61]

CATHEDRALS IMMEMORIAL

Sacred or secular, what is the difference? If every atom inside
our bodies was once a star, then it is all sacred and all
secular at the same time.

GRETEL EHRLICH, POET AND NOVELIST[1]

[S]tones, plants, animals, the earth, the sky, the stars, the elements,
in fact everything in the universe reveals to us the knowledge, power
and the will of its Originator.

ABU HAMID MUHAMMAD AL-GHAZZALI (1058–1111),
PERSIAN MYSTIC[2]

The Hooting Cairn

*M*arco Pallis, entomologist, mountain climber, sage, and music teacher of Greek parentage, addresses the metaphysical dimensions of the ageless cairn, a mound of stones erected as a marker or memorial that assists the seeker in achieving the heights of self-realization.

CAIRNS MARKING VARIOUS SPOTS of particular significance are among the most ancient and widely distributed monuments of human art; and the derivation of the word itself will suggest a reason. The primitive sense of the Celtic *carn* is "horn" (actually the same root) and the word is secondarily applied to any horn-like eminence, especially mountaintops. . . . The miniature cairn built of a pile of stones was used by the Celts and other peoples in order to mark sites of burial; the profound reasons for this practice are clear, since the cairn is itself an emblem of the Mountain of the Axis and fashioned on its model; it stands to serve as a perpetual reminder to the quick and the dead alike that the true Way, the direct route up the climb, must follow the axis, and that until the Goal has been attained by Knowledge, wayfaring must needs continue in this and other worlds.

In Tibet, for example, on reaching any high point occupied by a cairn, such as the crest of a pass, the traveller adds his stone to the pile with the ritual exclamation "the gods are victorious, all the devils are defeated," thus re-affirming his self-dedication in the Way; for in the larger sense the gods correspond to the higher possibilities of his being, and the devils to all those inferior tendencies that would drag him back and downward and that must be mastered and recalled to order if the Supreme Climb is ever to be completed.

The cairn is therefore the true image of the mountain pivot of the universe and provides, as it were, a preliminary vision of that which is presently to be realized. The building of a cairn "correctly" is indeed a ritual of the highest moment, whether this takes place at the foot or "gate" of the Way or, on completion of the ascent, upon the summit, where it symbolizes the "holy of holies," that is to say the Goal. In their outward form however the two cairns are indistinguishable so that, in one sense, whoever has contemplated the one with the "single eye" of understanding has likewise beheld the other.[3]

Pantheon

Whenever I go to foreign countries, I go and pay my respects to their temples, just as I do in Africa at those little heaps of stones which are the shrines of the Hottentots and the Bushmen. They move me very much, and I will add a stone to them as my contribution. The Hottentots put up these little stone piles to their god, 'Heitse Eibib', the god who fights the forces of darkness. This god they say, goes and fights for the power of light against the forces of the dark, and they say you can see him coming back from battle, bleeding in the red of the dawn, and you hear his voice in the rustling of the wind in the leaves of the trees. Wherever they crossed a river or stream they put down a stone in honour of the god and everybody who came by added a stone to it. The Hottentots have vanished, but these stone piles remain and these Hottentot churches, as I call them, in a strange way move me more than the great cathedrals have done.

LAURENS VAN DER POST, NOVELIST AND EXPLORER[4]

ack McPhee, Australian Aboriginal elder, describes the nature of sacred sites and the supernatural power stored in them and, by extension, invested in the surrounding landscape. They are embodiments of fertility—psychic, physical, and universal; hence the loss of any one site is experienced as an unspeakable sadness.

A SACRED SITE COULD BE A CAVE, rock, a pool, anywhere where a big snake could be or where he comes now and then. I'm not talking about a real snake in the sense of something you can see, I'm talking about a very old spiritual thing. I suppose a white person's sacred site might be his church, but you know when that church was built and you can feel it with your hands. Our sacred sites are more to do with the spirits, and they can't be dated because they've always been there.

There used to be a sacred site on the way back from the Comet mine, which is about six miles south-west of Marble Bar [in north-western Australia]. Just as you drive over the point of a big hill, there used to be a little bit of a creek that ran under a gum tree. It had been there for hundreds and hundreds and hundreds of years. When I was young you could always count on getting a drink of water there, even in drought time.

Unfortunately, white people didn't understand how special this place was. Someone went and dug a hole there, probably a prospector, hoping the water would build up, but of course it didn't, it just died away. You see, in doing that he killed Gadagadara, a snake with a strange head shaped like a horse's, who had placed his spirit there to live and keep the water for the people.

I remember the old ones being very upset when that site was destroyed. They had a meeting to try and work out who had killed Gadagadara, but no one knew. They were very sad for a long time after that.

There have been a number of places like that where I come from. In these special places there's been water, sometimes just a puddle, and then someone sends a grader in or someone tampers with it, and of course the water disappears because the spirit that kept it has been killed.[5]

Glastonbury Tor, Sacred Spiral Hill

*I*n the drama of the sweeping landscapes of East Africa, Carl Jung first became aware of his own awareness of the world. The Swiss psychiatrist writes of his experience of a "recognition of the immemorially known," which pervaded his journey through Africa. "A most intense *sentiment du déjà vu*" accompanied him, he says, in his travels across the continent. In 1925, while walking the Athi Plains of Kenya, the cosmic significance of consciousness was made "overwhelmingly clear" to him. Jung reflects upon this pivotal moment of stark enlightenment when he beheld the reality of the human psyche.

FROM NAIROBI WE USED A SMALL FORD to visit the Athi Plains, a great game preserve. From a low hill in this broad savanna a magnificent prospect opened out to us. To the very brink of the horizon we saw gigantic herds of animals: gazelle, antelope, gnu, zebra, warthog, and so on. Grazing, heads nodding, the herds moved forward like slow rivers. There was scarcely any sound save the melancholy cry of a bird of prey. This was the stillness of the eternal beginning, the world as it had always been, in the state of non-being; for until then no one had been present to know that it was this world. I walked away from my companions until I had put them out of sight, and savored the feeling of being entirely alone. There I was now, the first human being to recognize that this was the world, but who did not know that in this moment he had first really created it.

There the cosmic meaning of consciousness became overwhelmingly clear to me. . . . [M]an is indispensable for the completion of creation; that, in fact, he himself is the second creator of the world, who alone has given to the world its objective existence—without which, unheard, unseen, silently eating, giving birth, dying, heads nodding through hundreds of millions of years, it would have gone on in the profoundest night of non-being down to its unknown end. Human consciousness created objective existence and meaning, and man found his indispensable place in the great process of being.[6]

Buddha Nature

$\mathcal{I}$n an interview in 1984, the Venerable Tara Tulku, Rinpoche, one of the last monks to receive a complete Buddhist training in his native Tibet before the catastrophic 1959 Chinese invasion, commented on the intrinsic nature of sacredness and its relationship to place. How ground becomes holy is considered within the context of Sakyamuni Buddha's own metamorphosis at Bodhgaya, the Immovable Spot near Gaya on the floodplain of the Ganges in northeast India.

THE PLACE ITSELF, UNDER THE BODHI TREE at Bodhgaya, was transformed as well. It became a place of diamond, a *vajra* place, a place of extreme sacredness. Why is it sacred? Because Buddha's transformative experience of unexcelled perfect enlightenment blessed it in a special way. Some people even believe that if you reach and stand on that place and take the Bodhisattva vow or make prayers to achieve Buddhahood for the benefit of all beings, then just because of the power of that place, you will never be reborn in the lower states. And if you meditate there, recite prayers, and study, the place has a special power for the mind to come to realization. It is a place of light and bliss. This is because this is the place where Sakyamuni achieved the special Buddha body, a body which has only bliss and happiness, and never suffers. He also used this place as a basis for perceiving all places as indivisible from the highest heaven of the four realms. Because this place was the basis from which he re-envisioned all reality as the highest heaven, it is extremely sacred. . . .

Bodhgaya has a great special power infused in it by a person whose achievement was timeless, in the sense that the future was present. It lasts. Also, if one goes there with a strong vision of that moment, as if it were not separated from one, as if it were not past, then the power is much greater. But even when someone not thinking of its importance wanders through Bodhgaya, it has a very great power. Many people have remarked upon this. . . .

[M]y experiences at Bodhgaya . . . have been very powerful—praying, meditating, performing ceremonies. The tremendously peaceful atmosphere at Bodhgaya has had a great effect on me. It facilitates achieving my own sense of peacefulness. . . .

It doesn't matter what religion people hold, if they are going with an open mind, if they are seeking truth. In this case, it is extremely meritorious to go to the holy sites of any religion.[7]

One of the anchorites told this to the brothers in Rhaithou [in Sinai], the place where there were seventy palm trees and where Moses stopped with the people when they came out of the land of Egypt. He spoke thus: "I thought I would go into the inner desert on the chance that I might find someone who was living there before me and serving the Lord Christ. After travelling for four days and nights, I found a cave. Approaching it, I looked inside and saw a man seated. So I knocked, according to the custom of the monks, to make him come out and greet me. He did not move, for in fact he was dead. Unaware of this, I went in and touched his shoulder, and as I did so he crumbled into dust. I saw his tunic, and when I touched it, that too turned into nothing.

I was at quite a loss, and left there. I then found another cave and a human footprint. My hopes rose and I drew near to the cave. Again I knocked, and no one answered; when I entered, I found no one. I then stood outside of the cave and thought, "The servant of God has to come, wherever he may be." At the end of the day, I saw some antelopes coming, and the servant of God, naked. He had covered the unseemly parts of his body with his hair. As he came near me, he thought I was a spirit, and stopped to pray: he was, he said later, greatly tried by spirits. I realized this, and said to him, "I am a man, servant of God. See my footprints, and feel that I am flesh and blood." After his "Amen" he took a look at me and was reassured. Taking me into the cave, he said, "What brings you here?" I said, "I came into this desert to seek the servants of God. And I have not been disappointed in my wish."

THE WORLD OF THE DESERT FATHERS[8]

*P*hotographer and architect Thomas Miller ponders the ineffable legacy of the Colorado Plateau in the high desert of the American Southwest. Drawing upon the mystic chords of memory to plumb the meaning of desert without and within, Miller suggests that "the earth's skin may be more a muse than we know."

THE PLATEAU IS DEFINED by Precambrian faults half-a-billion years old. It is a microcosm of all that is extraordinary about the earth's crust. For me it is also a landscape of the mind and senses. Here, in the depths of solitude, I often see unexpected things and experience unexpected thoughts. . . .

I became aware of a communication between me and this desert skin and a feeling that I was not choosing my subjects so much as they were choosing me. . . .

Such thoughts accompanied a sense of eerie familiarity. I often felt I was looking at earth forms that are competent rough studies for the accoutrements of human civilization. The history of art is here, from figurative sculpture to abstract impressionism. Immense, silent cities of pyramids, ziggurats, temples, and cathedrals stand beside walls, arches, and domes, recording architectural history. Mathematics, from Euclid's geometries to networks and sets of a higher order, can also be discerned. Natural markings on stone suggest written language. Looking further, one sees a wheel, a gear, a knife blade. . . . Was our species given at birth a naturally formed blueprint for human invention? For human history? Have we spent the last ten thousand years (a relatively brief episode in our past) implementing this blueprint by creating the farms, towns, and other paraphernalia of civilization that so effectively insulate us from the landscape of our origins?[9]

Lizards in Love

The whale, like all things that are mighty, wears a false brow to the common world.

HERMAN MELVILLE (1819–1891)[10]

[N]o one with an unbiased mind can study any living creature, however humble, without being struck with enthusiasm at its marvellous structure and properties.

CHARLES DARWIN (1809–1882)[11]

$\mathcal{C}$harles Darwin and Herman Melville never met. Nonetheless, art historian and novelist Barbara Novak has ingeniously constructed a conversation that might have happened, by juxtaposing their thoughts in her gem of a book, *The Ape & The Whale*. Through an interplay of their mutually illuminating visions of the universe, immortality, nature, the Creator, and their own work, the ensuing dialogue is an engrossing piece of theater. It is also an eloquent meditation on the grand themes that have preoccupied the human species since time immemorial, through the eyes of two nineteenth-century geniuses, a scientist and an artist. Darwin and Melville both journeyed to the Galapagos; their explorations nearly overlapped: Darwin in 1835 and Melville in 1841. Each was fascinated, even mesmerized, by the islands' mammoth "antediluvian-looking" tortoises. "They seemed hardly of the seed of the earth," wrote Melville.

MELVILLE:
THESE MYSTIC CREATURES, suddenly translated by night from unutterable solitudes to our peopled deck, affected me in a manner not easy to unfold. They seemed newly crawled forth from beneath the foundations of the world. Yea, they seemed the identical tortoises whereon the Hindoo plants this total sphere. With a lantern I inspected them more closely. Such worshipful venerableness of aspect! Such furry greenness mantling the rude peelings and healing the fissures of their shattered shells. I no more saw three tortoises. They expanded—became transfigured. I seemed to see three Roman Coliseums in magnificent decay.

Ye oldest inhabitants of this or any other isle, said I, pray give me the freedom of your three-walled towns.

The great feeling inspired by these creatures was that of age:—dateless, indefinite endurance. And, in fact, that any other creature can live and breathe as long as the tortoise of the Encantadas, I will not readily believe. Not to hint of their known capacity of sustaining life, while going without food for an entire year, consider that impregnable armour of their living mail. What other bodily being possesses such a citadel wherein to resist the assaults of Time?

DARWIN:
THE TORTOISE IS VERY FOND OF water, drinking large quantities, and wallowing in the mud. The larger islands alone possess springs, and those are always situated towards the central parts, and at a considerable height. The tortoises, therefore, which frequent the lower districts, when thirsty, are obliged to travel from a long distance. Hence broad and well-beaten paths branch off in every direction from the wells down to the sea-coast; and the Spaniards by following them up, first discovered the watering-places. When I landed at Chatham Island, I could not imagine what animal travelled so methodically along well chosen paths. Near the springs it was a curious spectacle to behold many of these huge creatures, one set eagerly travelling onwards with outstretched necks, and another set returning, after having drunk their fill. When the tortoise arrives at the spring, quite regardless of any spectator, he buries his head in the water above his eyes, and greedily swallows great mouthfuls, at the rate of about ten a minute.[12]

The Hindus tell a story of a woman ascetic who once visited a particular temple in southern India. Exhausted from a long walk, she decided to rest beneath a tree near the entrance to the temple. As she was resting, one of the priests inside was shocked to observe the woman lying with her feet facing the temple, an act he considered highly disrespectful to the deity. When he pointed out her sacrilege, she replied, "Good sir, please inform me where God is not to be found, and I shall gladly place my feet in that direction."

AS RELATED BY CLIVE JAMES, IN HIS ANTHOLOGY *VEDANTA*[13]

*T*he whole thing is very much . . . a beautiful and holy vision,"[14] wrote Trappist monk Thomas Merton in his *Asian Journal*, recounting his visit to Polonnaruwa in Sri Lanka where the great stone buddhas stand and recline. "Those who carved those statues were not ordinary men," an Indian colleague told Merton while the monk from Gethsemani was attempting to explain his feelings about this twelfth-century sanctuary built by a Singhalese king.[15]

I AM ABLE TO APPROACH THE BUDDHAS barefoot and undisturbed, my feet in wet grass, wet sand. Then the silence of the extraordinary faces. The great smiles. Huge and yet subtle. Filled with every possibility, questioning nothing, knowing everything, rejecting nothing, the peace not of emotional resignation but of Madhyamika, of sunyata [emptiness, openness], that has seen through every question without trying to discredit anyone or anything. . . . I was knocked over with a rush of relief and thankfulness at the *obvious* clarity of the figures, the clarity and fluidity of shape and line, the design of the monumental bodies composed into the rock shape and landscape, figure, rock and tree. . . .

Looking at these figures I was suddenly, almost forcibly, jerked clean out of the habitual, half-tied vision of things, and an inner clearness, clarity, as if exploding from the rocks themselves, became evident and obvious. . . . The rock, all matter, all life, is charged with dharmakaya [the true nature of the Buddha, the essence of the universe] . . . everything is emptiness and everything is compassion. I don't know when in my life I have ever had such a sense of beauty and spiritual validity running together in one aesthetic illumination. . . . I don't know what else remains but I have now seen and have pierced through the surface and have got beyond the shadow and the disguise.[16]

Cornish Lingam

*T*homas Merton relates a comparable experience of Polonnaruwa after his visit to Mahabalipuram—a complex of cave shrines, monolithic rocks carved in bas-relief, and pagoda-like temples stretching out into the sea—built by the Pallava kings (A.D. 600–750) near Madras in south India. In an address to an interfaith conference in Calcutta, Merton explained the motivation for his journey to Asia: "I come as a pilgrim . . . to drink from ancient sources of monastic vision and experience."[17]

I HAVE SEEN THE SHIVA LINGAM [phallic form indicating the divine creative function of Shiva, an embodiment of eternal cosmic energy] at Mahabalipuram, standing black and alone at the edge of the ocean, washed by spray of great waves breaking on the rocks.

> He stands like a lighthouse, night churns
> Round his base, his dark light rolls
> Into darkness, and darkly returns.
> Is he calling, the lone one? Is his deep
> Silence full of summons?

There is no "problem," however, in the black lingam. It is washed by the sea, and the sea is woman: it is no void, no question. No English anguish about Mahabalipuram. How right the "lighthouse" stanza of Lawrence [D. H.] is, though, for this lingam on the rocky point!

Mahabalipuram is the remains of a culture such as I have not seen before. A complex of shrines carved out of, or built into, a great ancient rock formation—not cliffs but low rambling outcrops and boulders, smoothed and shaped by millions of years. Caves, porches, figures, steps, markings, lines of holes, gods and goddesses. . . .

Surely, with Mahabalipuram and Polonnaruwa my Asian pilgrimage has become clear and purified itself. I mean, I know and have seen what I was obscurely looking for.[18]

*I*n their fascinating account of a man and a tree—the remarkable Allen Meredith and his beloved yew—authors Anand Chetan and Diana Brueton rediscover through the work of Meredith the influence of the yew on the construction of megalithic sites circa 2800 B.C.

A LARGE PART OF THE YEW'S SUCCESS [as a species] must lie in its extraordinary ability to regenerate itself. Left undisturbed for millennia, the branches root in the earth, producing widening circles of new trees and forming what must have appeared to early peoples as vast natural cathedrals—the sacred groves. Remaining green throughout the long winter, these sanctuaries were both the place for and the object of the earliest human impulses to worship. Allen believes that when our prehistoric ancestors built sacred sites such as Stonehenge and nearby Woodhenge, constructed from concentric circles of posts, the circular design was determined at least in part by a desire to re-create the yew grove.[19]

*E*ven a modernized Muslim experiences deep down in his heart the sense of peace and joy, even a kind of psychological 'assurance,' when sitting on a traditional carpet, viewing a piece of calligraphy, or hearing classical poetry of his or her language, not to speak of hearing the Quranic psalmody or praying within the confines of one of the masterpieces of Islamic architecture," writes the distinguished Islamic scholar and teacher Seyyed Hossein Nasr.[20] Islamic sacred art for Nasr represents "a descent of heavenly reality upon the earth." It can range from traditional music, architecture, and literature to miniatures, pottery, or an arabesque. Professor Nasr provides us with but one example of this profoundly rich variety of forms, colors, and sounds that "serve as vehicles for the attainment of that Truth (*al-Haqq*) which is at once Majesty (*al-Jalal*) and Beauty (*al-Jamal*)."[21]

[S]ANCTIFICATION OF THE GROUND by the very act of the *sujud* [prostration] of the Blessed Prophet . . . bestowed a new meaning upon the ground and the carpet covering it. The carpet, whether of simple white colour or full of geometric and arabesque patterns and ornaments, reflects Heaven and enables the traditional Muslim who spends most of his time at home on the carpet to experience the ground upon which he sits as purified and participating in the sacred character of the ground of the mosque upon which he prays. . . .

The traditional carpet is the earthly reflection of the cosmos itself. To sit upon it is to be located within a sacred precinct protected by its borders and often looking inward towards the centre where all the patterns meet. . . .[22]

Elves in the Tree

$\mathcal{T}$ewa architectural historian Rina Swentzell, of Santa Clara Pueblo in New Mexico, describes the nature of sacred space in Pueblo society. It is an interdimensional universe where a vast inclusiveness interlocks all.

LAST SUMMER AS I STOOD on top of one of Santa Clara Pueblo's sacred mountains, I was most impressed by the wind, the beauty of the clouds and the flow of the hills below. There is a shrine on top of that mountain with a few well-placed stones which define an area scattered with cornmeal and a deeply-worn path in the bedrock. No special structure celebrates the sacredness of this place. Architecturally, it is understated, almost inconspicuous. That particular shrine is typical of Pueblo shrines in that it is visually disappointing. It is, nevertheless, a very special place because it is a place of access to the underworld from which Pueblo People emerged. It is a doorway of communication between the many simultaneous levels of Pueblo existence.

Understanding the visual understatement of that shrine is important to understanding Pueblo sacred space. Visually and physically understated shrines, or, for that matter, Pueblo community and house forms stem from the very nature of Pueblo cosmology. At the center of the Pueblo belief system is the conviction that people are not separate from nature and natural forces. This insoluble connection with nature has existed from the beginning of time. The goal of human existence is to maintain wholeness or oneness with the natural universe.[23]

Wishing Stone

*A*ncient traditional texts called *Lontar,* inscribed in old Balinese and old Javanese and said to have originated from Sanskrit literature, demonstrate how the physical and metaphysical universes merge. At death, for example, the body—composed of the elements of earth, air, water, and fire—joins its corresponding points of origin. The soul, for its part, will reincarnate or commingle with the Eternal Soul. The palm-leaf manuscripts (palm leaves that have been dried, treated, and bound) reflect the mutuality of all life, the body being the microcosm, the ultimate temple. They also specify one's place and makeup in the organic structure of the universe.

- The physical body (*badan*) turns to earth,
- body hair (*bulu*) to shrubs,
- the skin (*kulit*) to earth,
- the muscles (*daging*) to clay,
- the tendons (*otot*) to branches of vegetation,
- the spinal cord (*sam-sam*) to the axis of the earth,
- the eyes (*mata*) to the sun or the moon,
- the head (*kepala*) to the sky,
- the life force or vital power (*bayu*) to the wind,
- the voice (*soara*) to thunder,
- the liver (*hati*) to fire,
- the heart (*jantung*) to a mountain,
- the pulma (*paru-paru*) to red clouds in the sky,
- the bowels (*usus*) to sunrays,
- the kidneys (*ungsilan*) to stone,
- the spleen (*limpa*) to a shining lake,

- the tissue of the bowels (*dujaringan*) to rain,
- the sour gall (*ampu*) to energy or power,
- the intestines (*ineban*) to the ocean,
- the stomach (*perut*) to crater,
- the hair (of the head) (*rambut*) to dew,
- the sexual organs (*kemalwar*) to the God and Goddess of Love Hyang Semare and Hyang Semari,
- the sperms (*kama*) to their godly origins as Brahma, Vishnu, and Shiva,
- the senses (*rasa*) to salt.[24]

Languorous Nude

In 1869 Major J. Wesley Powell, a geologist and one-armed veteran of the Civil War, ensconced in a seat strapped to the deck of a small boat, descended into the unknown canyons of the Green, Grand, and Colorado rivers (of Utah, Colorado, and Arizona). Despite the dangers of the dizzying velocity of unimaginable rapids, extremes of heat and cold, and the loss of life, he would write of the imperative of wilderness as essential to the flourishing of the human spirit. Powell knew the inner gorge of the Grand Canyon—in its terror, in its exaltation of divinity. It was a gift that was earned.

THE GLORIES AND THE BEAUTIES OF FORM, color and sound unite in the Grand Canyon—forms unrivaled even by the mountains, colors that vie with sunsets, and sounds that span the diapason from tempest to tinkling raindrop, from cataract to bubbling fountain. . . .

You cannot see the Grand Canyon in one view, as if it were a changeless spectacle from which a curtain might be lifted, but to see it you have to toil from month to month through its labyrinths. It is a region more difficult to traverse than the Alps or the Himalayas, but if strength and courage are sufficient for the task, by a year's toil a concept of sublimity can be obtained never again to be equaled on the hither side of Paradise.[25]

Chun Quoit

$\mathcal{I}$n his record of a search, a journey "to a larger frame of human existence," Ghanaian poet, statesman, and novelist Kofi Awoonor takes us to the holy center of his people, the Anlo-Ewe of Ghana in west Africa. The nature and mystery of this spiritual locus have constituted the religious and social underpinnings of Awoonor's inspiring life, beginning with his first awakening.

MY MOTHER TELLS THE STORY of my birth, of how, for a significant and ominous period after my delivery I did not emit a sound or show any sign of life. An old woman, an accomplished healer, was summoned. I was rushed to the family ancestral shrine, *Togbuizikpuixo* at Weta in the southern Volta Region of Ghana. It was there I came to life.

That shrine still stands, a spiritual refuge for many hundreds with whom I share a common ancestry. The mystery that it evokes, its power and role in the lives of the family including my own life, constitute the main focus of our collective religious consciousness. Around this shrine is constructed a set of immutable moral laws, taboos, rituals and ceremonies. It is the beginning and the end, the point of departure and return for many of us.

The shrine has been the center of my life for many years. I have been back during my early school years, tugging on my mother's cloth, and relishing the meals we shared with the illustrious ones. I have gone there on the eve of long journeys, and on return from them went back to salute and thank the ancestors with the obligatory ram and drinks.

The shrine is a simple structure, once built of mud and thatched with *ebe*, the common wet-land grass still used in thatching houses throughout Ghana; it is now rebuilt with cement and roofed with aluminum. My family belongs to this shrine by direct maternal descendance.

Among the Anlo-Ewe, just as among many African peoples, *ancestralism* is part of the religious system of the people. The dead assume responsibility for those they have left behind. Crucially, they are in direct contact with all the higher spirit forces of the universe, and consequently with the Supreme Being Him/Her Self. They act as intermediaries, interveners and interpreters between the living, to whom they are still linked by blood, and the spirit forces whose world they share in their condition.

The ancestors are therefore invoked on all important occasions. The shrine serves as the focal point for the clan and the family's religious life. Each member of the clan, on the eve of a special journey or an important undertaking—whether it is the preparation and planting of a new farm or the start of a new business—can go to the guardian-priest of the shrine (who is my maternal uncle) and ask that the shrine's "doors be opened for him." The supplicant brings with him a young ram, a few bottles of assorted drinks including an obligatory local gin, some yards of white calico and at times some money.

On the dawn of the day the guardian-priest of the shrine assigns to the supplicant, a number of family and clan members gather for the ceremony. The various items requisitioned are on display. The ram is slaughtered and the carcass, still dripping with blood, is held over effigies of the ancestors by the guardian-priest.

The carcass is cut into pieces, and a special meal is prepared made of fresh dried corn powder which is eaten with the meat. The supplicant is now invited to come into the shrine, walking in backwards, stripped of all his clothes except the undergarment. He is made to kneel before the platform on which the ancestral effigies are placed. The guardian-priest then introduces the supplicant and the reason why he has asked for the shrine's "door to be opened for him." He then asks the supplicant to present his own case. The supplicant then shares the meal with the ancestors.

Outside, the feasting has already begun. Children, the old, every member of the clan come to partake of the sacred meal. This provides an occasion for communal conviviality, sharing and laughter. Drinks are served liberally. Some of the old folks get properly drunk by the end of the feast. By early noon, all is over and the supplicant and his entourage are given permission to leave. The following year, when the harvest is good, the supplicant will return with abundant gift offerings. People do not go to the shrine only to ask for help. They also go there to give thanks.

It is fascinating to witness the depth of belief and trust reposited by every clan or family member in the power of this shrine. By its intervening, healing and protective power, this shrine remains one of the most active spiritual centers in my town of Weta. My relationship with it is privileged because it has always been under the priestly guardianship of three successive maternal uncles.[26]

Indian Head

Indians in Manhattan [have] been here since long before the buildings and will be here long after the buildings are gone. . . . I always think when you see that stone-faced Indian, what's on his mind is that there's something really funny he just heard.

OREN LYONS, FAITHKEEPER OF THE
TURTLE CLAN OF THE ONONDAGA NATION[27]

*M*atsuo Bashō experiences an epiphany at a sacred rock shrine near the pinnacle of a mountain in Yamagata in northern Japan.

THERE WAS A TEMPLE called Ryushakuji in the province of Yamagata. Founded by the great Priest Jikaku [in A.D. 860), this temple was known for the absolute tranquillity of its holy compound. Since everybody advised me to see it, I changed my course at Obanazawa and went there, though it meant walking an extra seven miles or so. When I reached it, the late afternoon sun was still lingering over the scene. After arranging to stay with the priests at the foot of the mountain, I climbed to the temple situated near the summit. The whole mountain was made of massive rocks thrown together, and covered with age-old pines and oaks. The stony ground itself bore the colour of eternity, paved with velvety moss. The doors of the shrines built on the rocks were firmly barred and there was not a sound to be heard. As I moved on all fours from rock to rock, bowing reverently at each shrine, I felt the purifying power of this holy environment pervading my whole being.[28]

A Congregation of Animal Spirits (Series #1–5)

$\mathcal{S}$omewhere between A.D. 460 and 465 work was begun on a series of spectacular sculptures that erupted into a riot of form and scale and a blaze of color that is almost unsurpassed in the worlds of archaeological and spiritual treasures. Out of a sandstone cliff at Yunkang in Shanxi, near the northern Wei capital at Datong, five richly carved cave temples were hewn in commemoration of earlier kings of the northern Wei dynasty, which ruled much of northern China from A.D. 385 TO 534. Over the course of the next thirty years, numerous cave temples were constructed; some forty have survived, but it is the first twenty that astound. They record the preliminary incursions of Buddhism in northern China with the accompanying artistic flourishes that marked Buddhist iconography. The colossal dimensions of some of the images—ranging in height from forty to fifty feet—puts them in a class of their own. Buddhist monk John Blofeld describes this wild congregation of buddhas and bodhisattvas, heavenly musicians and swarming winged messengers along with innumerable deities with multiple heads, legs, and arms, which he encountered on one of his pilgrimages through northern China in the early part of this century. He could think of nothing in China that exceeded the Yunkang rock carvings "in their power to evoke absolute certainty of a lovely and eternal Reality underlying the world of appearances."[29]

THE YUNKANG CAVES . . . are among the few places in the world which cannot possibly disappoint even the more extravagant expectations. It is now thought that Buddhism first trickled into China as far back as the second century B.C. By the time these cave temples were hewn from the living rock in the fifth, sixth and seventh centuries A.D., the Indian religion was spreading like a bright flame across the face of Asia. The men who came in contact with it then were inspired with a great upsurge of the spirit comparable to that which led to the building of Europe's loveliest cathedrals. . . . In each cave, the principal Buddha-image (formed by cutting the rock from around it on three or four sides) is so enormous that, in at least one case, I estimated the nose alone to be twice as long as my six-foot body—perhaps much more than that, for it is difficult to judge the length of something high above one's head. . . .

The staggering size of these images strikes the mind with wonder as soon as the caves are entered; but, before long, this wonder is thrust into the background by the even more astounding *beauty* of the sculpture, especially of the thousands of small figures surrounding the giant images. For centuries, these great statues have sat silently brooding on human sorrows, their lips touched with the faintest of compassionate smiles—but not in solitude. In each cave, walls and ceiling are a mass of intricate carvings. Buddhas, Bodhisattvas, devas, asparas [winged messengers], a host of spiritual beings—thousands upon thousands of them in every cave—stare down at the puny descendants of their inspired creators. Some reflect the brooding calm of the central images; others are running, leaping, flying, dancing, singing, twanging stringed instruments, blowing on horns, waving their arms, flapping their wings, making faces, rocking with laughter in so lively a manner that it is hard not to believe they are living beings petrified by a magician's spell.

I never thought it possible that inanimate beauty could be so moving.[30]

Womb

I am looking for the cave tree, a tree I once encountered by accident. Underneath this large redwood there is a small dirt chamber big enough to stand in. The entrance is easy to miss; the tree looks as solid as any other from a distance. I ache to climb into this secret hollow today and hide from the world of thoughtless violence. I want to go deep into the earth and sit in the roots of a Tall One. I am hungry for the stillness and wisdom of caves.

STEPHANIE KAZA[31]

James Cowan stumbled upon an Aboriginal sculpture made of sand in northern Australia that caused in him a shift in consciousness and lifted him to a more luminous realm. Cowan has traveled vast distances in his thirst for sapience. The *djel*, an ancient mythological map associated with mortuary rites, was but one portal along the way—a metaphysical route to what's immortal within him.

I WAS FASCINATED by the symmetry of these sand ridges. Nowhere before I had ever encountered such a careful execution of an image which was obviously derived from a different order of experience altogether. You see, the sand sculpture partook of something I could only assume was *sublime*. The journey that it explored reminded me of Dante's words when he remarked, "I had set foot in that part of life beyond which one cannot go with any hope of returning." Here, in the sand, was a striking physical resemblance to the great poet's trek up Mount Purgatory in his quest of paradise. How else can I describe to you the maze-like corridors, the feeling of *entry* that the *djel* conveyed? Indeed, I might have been mistaken in believing that what lay before me was the plan of a Sakkaran pyramid outside Memphis, with its narrow tunnels leading to the hallowed tomb of the mummy. My Yolngu friends had constructed a pure, geomantic design in keeping with some of the great mystical edifices of mankind. I was left with the inescapable conclusion these tribesmen were in possession of the archetype of all mystical edifices to which we are heirs. There seemed to be no accident that in each *djel* I subsequently viewed, the plan of Chartres, the Taj Mahal, Angkor Wat, even the sacred Egyptian hieroglyph itself, found its prototype. And when I later studied a sand sculpture, shaped by another clan member for a washing ceremony following the death of a friend, I knew I was looking at the emerging shape of the Egyptian hieroglyph *ankh*, meaning "life."

I have seen a sand sculpture for a smoke ceremony which is shaped like a Viking grave site. Another washing ceremony *djel* I witnessed duplicated almost exactly a Byzantine cross from the cathedral of Cosenza. Such shapes in the sand only made me realise I had stumbled among a variety of configurations whose origins were metaphysical rather than psychological. Like Dante, I had embarked upon a journey from which there was no likelihood of return. Each *djel* was the reflection of the spiritual *condition* of the deceased, and served to ensure the journey his spirit made was in accordance with his clan and totemic existence when alive.

Where does all this leave me, you may ask? In a state of amazement, mostly! It's one thing to go for a walk along the beach in search of solitude; quite another to find oneself surrounded by the hieratic moments in a man's inner journey. We gaze in awe at tomb reliefs in Egypt, or mandalas in Tibet, depicting transitionary stages in the journey of a departing soul for the other world, and of course respect their hieratic dignity. How much more poignant it is to discover these same icons laid out in the sand at your feet by friends you know! And to think the tide will soon wash them away and so erase what had earlier been an *inner* experience. Clearly, the mind is neither so pure nor so idolatrous that it can dismiss the walls of its tombs in an act of transcendence. Otherwise what point is there in ritually washing the body at the centre of one of these sand sculptures?[32]

Stonehenge

When the Romans sought to punish the Carthaginians for disobedience by razing their city to the ground, citizens of Carthage begged their masters to spare the physical city, its stones and temples, to which no possible guilt could be attached, and instead, if necessary, exterminate the entire population.

YI-FU TUAN, CULTURAL GEOGRAPHER AND WRITER[33]

*T*he stone temples and mountain fastnesses of Tibet shape a landscape that "appears like the organic expression of primeval forces," writes the Buddhist scholar, painter, and spiritual leader Lama Anagarika Govinda in his autobiographical account of his years of seeking and yearning in the unknown regions beyond the Himalayas. In 1933 as he is about to complete the final ascent of an eighteen-thousand-foot pass, he encounters timeless manifestations of the divine at work and play.

LATE IN THE AFTERNOON we reached the entrance of a gorge from which the final ascent of the pass was to start. At the foot of a group of ragged rocks, piled one upon the other on the flank of a steep mountain, there appeared to be a few stone hovels, whose cubic forms were hardly distinguishable from the tumbled rocks. A strange contrast, however, was provided by innumerable whitewashed *chorten*, religious monuments which have their origin in the ancient *stupas* of India, consisting of a cubic base, a hemispherical or vase-shaped middle piece, and a long conical spire of brick-red disks, crowned with the symbols of sun and moon.

Millions of such monuments are scattered all over Tibet. They are found wherever human beings live or have lived, and even on dangerous passes, at the entrances of precariously constructed suspension bridges, or on strange rock formations near the caravan routes. The great number of *chortens* which appeared here, as if the rocks had been transformed into these shapes by magic, indicated the vicinity of a temple or a monastery. As I had heard of a very ancient rock monastery, situated in one of the gorges of these mountains, I followed the narrow path leading through the *chortens*, and soon I found myself in a maze of huge boulders and towering rock-walls. . . .

I climbed on through a labyrinth of rocks and buildings. . . . Near each entrance I observed a small stone pyramid, and each of them was crowned with a flat, plate-like stone slab, upon which a small round stone had been placed. I was about to ask the one of my two men, who had accompanied me, while the other had remained behind with the horses, whether these structures were a kind of miniature *chorten*, when he picked up one of the small round stones and let it fall upon the slab, from which he had taken it. The slab emitted a clear, glassy sound. So this was the house-bell! I could not help admiring the ingenuity of these simple people. . . .

[A]n old friendly looking Lama . . . welcomed me with great politeness. I told him that I was a pilgrim from a far-off country, and, seeing my monastic robes, he opened without hesitation the heavy door at the base of the rock temple and beckoned me to follow him.

He led me through a steep, dark staircase into a big cave. The smooth walls were covered with apparently very ancient frescoes. In the mellow light of an altar-lamp I could see the statue of the great Buddhist Apostle Padmasambhava, the founder of the Old Sect (Nying-ma-pa), to which this monastery belonged. The image was flanked by two statues of Bodhisattvas and Padmasambhava's two chief disciples, the Indian princess Mandarava and the Tibetan incarnate *Khadoma*. . . . [34]

*I*n his meditation on the holy Koran (*The Heart of the Koran*)—the living revelation from which all the dimensions of Muslim civilization and spiritual life issue—author, scholar, and teacher of mystical Islam Lex Hixon describes his pilgrimage to the holy city of Mecca in Arabia to circumambulate the holy Ka'bah, the sacred shrine, the House of Allah—the center of spiritual power and inspiration for the Islamic world. Hixon traveled with, among others, his close friend and Sufi master, Sheikh Muzaffer, Grand Sheikh and renowned leader of the Halveti-Jerrahi Order of Dervishes and proprietor of a small shop in the Istanbul bazaar. Over the course of a week, they joined some three million other Muslims from across the planet in the traditional and potent sacrament of *hadjj* (pilgrimage) to bathe in the purifying radiance of the Divine Presence. Hixon's experience dramatizes the mystical function of pilgrimage, which allows us, he writes, "to experience death and the Day of Resurrection" while still on this earth. Hixon is immersed in the metaphysical landscape of holy ground as he completes one stage of his journey.

THE NEXT NIGHT we made our third and farewell *Tawaf*, consisting of seven circumambulations of the Holy Ka'bah. In the center of the huge white marble courtyard within the grand mosque in Mecca stands the cubic structure, covered with rich black cloth, that represents the axis of the world. Islamic tradition tells us that this sacred cube was first built by the Prophet Adam, was constructed again after millennia by the Prophet Abraham, and was then renewed and rededicated to the One God by the Prophet Muhammad. The inspiration of this vast and powerful prophetic lineage tangibly irradiates the atmosphere.

Since the ever-present Source is formless, there are no images within or around this shrine. Its radiant blackness symbolizes the unimaginable holy mystery. The Divine Radiance here is too intense to experience as light. The mystic blackness is more luminous than that which exists beneath the surface of the sun.

Lost in an ecstatic whirlpool of several hundred thousand human forms, we are drawn closer and closer toward the axis of Being where the Divine Transcendence fully intersects with our planetary dimension of existence. Muslims from cultures throughout the earth are facing toward this center of the world, the Holy Ka'bah, as they perform their daily prayers, thereby transforming the entire planet into a sacred mosque.

Barefoot on cool marble, in the hours after midnight, we are swept round and round this central pole of manifestation. There are no tears, no insights, no visions. The essence of reality revealed here is too transcendent to be rendered into the language of the senses, mind, or heart. Only the secret soul knows what is here, that reality which neither words nor even experience can express. The true Ka'bah is none other than the diamond essence of the soul, the Muhammad of Light, the Logos who is simply Allah knowing Allah.

Following this final *Tawaf*, we returned as pure as newborn infants to the school outside Mecca where we were staying. We drank tea, performed the dawn prayers, and plunged into sleep. I dreamed for hours that I was repeating '*Ya Salaam, Ya Salaam, Ya Salaam*'—one of the ninety-nine Koranic Names of Allah meaning, *Thou All-Peaceful One*. Drifting into the waking world, I could see my pilgrim brothers asleep on their mats around me and could clearly perceive that Divine Peace was descending not just upon me, but upon them and the whole world.[35]

Sea Lion

I sometimes choose to think that man is a dream, thought an illusion, and only rock is real. Rock and sun . . . belief? What do I believe in? I believe in sun. In rock. In the dogma of the sun and the doctrine of the rock.

EDWARD ABBEY, DESERT ANARCHIST,
AUTHOR, AND TWENTIETH-CENTURY POLEMICIST[36]

OPEN-AIR CATHEDRALS

Space has a spiritual equivalent and can heal what is divided
and burdensome in us.

GRETEL EHRLICH, POET, NOVELIST, AND RANCHER[1]

Sacred places are the truest definitions of the earth. They stand for the
earth immediately and forever; they are its flags and its shields.
If you would know the earth for what it really is, learn it through
its sacred places.

N. SCOTT MOMADAY, KIOWA NOVELIST AND PAINTER[2]

Tregeseal Circle

*I*diosyncratic naturalist Edward Abbey (1927–1989) leaves us in no doubt as to the transcendent value of wilderness.

WILDERNESS. THE WORD ITSELF IS MUSIC.

Wilderness, wilderness. . . . We scarcely know what we mean by the term, though the sound of it draws all whose nerves and emotions have not yet been irreparably stunned, deadened, numbed by the caterwauling of commerce, the sweating scramble for profit and domination.

Why such allure in the very word? What does it really mean? Can wilderness be defined in the words of government officialdom as simply "A minimum of not less than 5,000 contiguous acres of roadless area"? This much may be essential in attempting a definition but it is not sufficient; something more is involved.

Suppose we say that wilderness invokes nostalgia, a justified not merely sentimental nostalgia for the lost America our forefathers knew. The word suggests the past and the unknown, the womb of earth from which we all emerged. It means something lost and something still present, something remote and at the same time intimate, something buried in our blood and nerves, something beyond us and without limit. Romance—but not to be dismissed on that account. The romantic view, while not the whole of truth, is a necessary part of the whole truth.

But the love of wilderness is more than a hunger for what is always beyond reach; it is also an expression of loyalty to the earth, the earth which bore us and sustains us, the only home we shall ever know, the only paradise we ever need—if only we had the eyes to see . . . if only we were worthy of it.[3]

Theologian Belden C. Lane describes a reckoning in self-perception when he unexpectedly encounters a deer in a small, wooded clearing on the bluffs overlooking the Mississippi River in Pere Marquette State Park, Illinois. Resting for an indefinite time against a fallen tree, Lane is jolted, without warning, out of a contented reverie into a crystalline attunement to Spirit.

[S]UDDENLY I HEARD SOMETHING in the brush to my right. The sound was different from the others, heavier. I knew it was made by something more conscious than the smaller creatures around. I felt not only its weight but also its consciousness—its frightening likeness to myself. A person, I thought, or a dog. Then I saw it. For some time I thought it was a large dog, or some animal I couldn't name. (As I think of it now, the lack of a name was what formed so much of the mystery I felt.) It was a deer, a young doe, I think.

Staying perfectly still, I breathed as lightly as possible, my warm breath nevertheless smoking around my face in the cold air. Gradually, the deer made its way right into the clearing where I had been waiting. In fact, she reached the very point where I had first been looking to meet something long moments before, when suddenly she saw me. She stopped fast, stamping her right front hoof, moving her head up and down, then from side to side, studying me intently. She wagged her white tail fiercely and seemed to gaze through me with those large, dark eyes. For a moment she jumped back into the brush, but I waited, and soon she came back out, eyeing me carefully but walking on in the direction she had been heading.

Down the slope to water, no doubt. I watched until she disappeared.

A simple, utterly peaceful and mysterious meeting it had been. The uncanny thing was that I had been invited to the place, I had felt the deer (I felt some presence) in the clearing a good ten or fifteen minutes *before* she came. I somehow *knew* that if I just were still and waited, there would be a meeting. It was a gift, and a strange conclusion to the whole day's experience. Having spent the day searching for mana, for mystic voices, a luminous encounter with the Other, I met simply a deer. Walking back home, toward the vanishing red sunset, with honking geese passing high overhead, I felt an enormous joy.[4]

*P*oet and novelist Gretel Ehrlich lives on a ranch in Wyoming, an "end-of-the-road place" isolated by the ten-thousand-foot mountains that rise behind it; a place where "dinosaurs came and went." Ehrlich reflects upon the ways in which we come to recognize the nature of sacred ground.

TO SEE MEANS TO STOP, to breathe in and out. John Muir [botanist and conservationist] considered studying the history of a single rain-drop for the rest of his life. To see and to know a place is a contempla-tive act. It means emptying our minds and letting what is there, in all its multiplicity and endless variety, come in. We talk about looking into someone's eyes as "seeing into" them. Why not look "into" the earth? If John Muir had pursued his study of the raindrop, he would have discovered the entire natural world. . . .

The root word in "religion" means "to bind." It is no mere coin-cidence that our feelings about a place take on spiritual dimensions. An old rancher once told me he thought the lines in his hand had come directly up from the earth, that the land had carved them there after so many years of work. We are bound to place. The Japanese poet and priest Ikkyu referred to any passionate connection as "red threads." Perhaps it is red thread that holds me here in Wyoming.

The ways in which we come to know a landscape are preliterate. "A sense of place" implies a sensory knowledge. It mounts up in our minds: empires of smells and sounds, textures and sights held fast by memory, flooding back again and again in such urgent, pungent ways as to let us reenter those places. A river slits its neck for us; the eerie sound a sandhill crane makes comes into our human throats as song; in the mountain fastness of granite cracks, a pine tree grows; and we humans dive backward and forward in time, beginning seventy million years ago, when the mountains came into being. We rise with the landforms. We feel the upper altitudes of thin air, sharp stings of snow and ultraviolet on our flesh. . . .

All during our lives, in any and every place we live or visit, the sacramental landscape unrolls before us. It is our text. It is public and private, social and wild, political and aesthetic. To see—that is, to discover—is not an act of interpretation, of transfixing with preconceived ideas what is before us; rather, it is an act of surrender.[5]

*A*rtist, poet, statesman, scientist, and author Chiang Yee signs his paintings with the pen name "The Silent Priest," yet he manages to give us a provocative and entertaining interpretation of the history, principles, and philosophy of Chinese painting in *The Chinese Eye*. He writes that Chinese painting may be viewed as synonymous with culture, so closely are its origins, rise, and disposition related to the common thought of any given time—wherein the essence of Nature predominates and prevails.

WE LOVE NATURE; we consider human beings as but one small part of all created things. We feel that the original good and simple character of man has been gradually lost in the progress of civilisation, and so we shift our affection toward other parts of the universe. Especially we love animals, birds, fish, and flowers, and you find these more frequently than the human form as subjects of Chinese paintings. We love birds particularly; sometimes in China you will see a man carrying a cage, or with a bird perched on his shoulder, taking his pet for an airing, just as you take your dogs for a run. We take them for a slow stroll in the forest, we put them in a cage and hang it in the trees to let them sing with their companions of the forest, and answer them. We sit down and listen to their singing. We cannot pretend to run as fast as dogs, and so we find birds more companionable.

As I have tried to show, we love natural truth; our philosophers were convinced that human desire has grown beyond bounds; man's eagerness to grasp the object of his desire gives rise to much unnatural and untruthful behaviour. Man, we think, is no higher in the scale of things than any other kind of matter that comes into being; rather, he has tended to falsify his original nature, and for that reason we prefer those things that live by instinct or natural compulsion; they are at least true to the purpose for which they were created. We paint figures occasionally, but not so much as you do in the West. . . .

Our love of Nature is based upon a desire to identify our minds with her and to enjoy her as she is.[6]

Peak Experience

Tell me the landscape in which you live and I will tell you who you are.

JOSÉ ORTEGA Y GASSET (1883–1955),
SPANISH PHILOSOPHER[7]

Landscape: what you see in yourself.

Self-portrait: how you want others to see you.

Figure: better to talk to than to draw.

Still life: something that moves too fast to capture.

KAZUAKI TANAHASHI, ZEN PAINTER, CALLIGRAPHER, AND TEACHER[8]

The beautiful landscape

   as we know

   belongs to those who are like it.

MUSO SOSEKI (1275–1351), ZEN MONK AND POET[9]

*E*dward Abbey has spent his life divining the mystique of the desert of the American Southwest, ultimately abandoning all efforts to understand it. The corpus of his work suggests that all would-be answers are fraught with paradox. On a boat trip down Glen Canyon in Utah, Abbey pauses for a hike up the gorge of the Escalante. Entranced by the improbable grandeur of the canyon's stratified brilliance, Abbey experiences a brief shower of preternatural grace.

IS THIS AT LAST THE LOCUS DEI? There are enough cathedrals and temples and altars here for a Hindu pantheon of divinities. Each time I look up one of the secretive little side canyons I half expect to see not only the cottonwood tree rising over its tiny spring—the leafy god, the desert's liquid eye—but also a rainbow-colored corona of blazing light, pure spirit, pure being, pure disembodied intelligence, *about to speak my name.*

If a man's imagination were not so weak . . . he would learn to perceive in water, leaves, and silence more than sufficient of the absolute and marvelous, more than enough to console him for the loss of the ancient dreams.[10]

Wolf Emergent

Ridge after ridge and peak after peak there are;

From afar or near-by, from above or below, each has

a different form.

The true features of Lu Mountains cannot be recognised,

Because we ourselves are always engulfed in these

mountains.

SU TUNG-P'O (SUNG DYNASTY, A.D. 960–1276),

POET, PAINTER, ESSAYIST,

HUMORIST, AND CALLIGRAPHIST[11]

Hoh Gargoyle

Oren Lyons, Faithkeeper of the Turtle Clan of the Onondaga Nation, sets the record straight on the real value of Manhattan and the true nature of the Dutch real estate deal.

MANHATTAN WAS A BEAUTIFUL PLACE. It was the best fishing and hunting grounds in the East. People came here in the seasons to hunt and fish. And you could in a day or two, you could get enough game to last you the winter. If there was a gift that we gave to the white man it was the concept of "free" and "how to be free." That's what they found here. When they asked if they could buy Manhattan—well, of course! How could you talk a concept of buy and sell with a people who didn't have that concept. All of the native people understood that this was a neutral ground and a ground where people shared—that the idea of our white brothers coming across the sea would be welcome here. And if they chose to give a small gift for that, that was fine, that was nice, that had appreciation. And so the consequence of that was, what they call, the sale of Manhattan. And we still hear about that today. There's a lot of laughter involved that you sold Manhattan for twenty gilders, and we say well we don't understand that—but nevertheless we think at the time what was struck was an agreement to share something. When the Indians returned the next year they found fences and they said "What is this?" We're coming back to fish and hunt. They said—well—you sold it. What do you mean we sold it!

This [Manhattan] was once covered with great pines; there were great forests here. We had a meeting at the Cathedral of St. John the Divine and I reminded them that there *was* a cathedral here that was much larger and that was *the cathedral of pines*. They towered two hundred, two hundred and fifty feet into the air. That was the cathedral, if you will, of how Indians think. The sky is our roof, the earth our floor, and everything in between is bountiful for us.[12]

Tree Angel

In a rhapsodic flight, AE (pen name of Irish poet, painter, and journalist George William Russell) recalls a moment when he experienced a striking epiphany regarding the mystery and mystique of the Emerald Isle.

LAST YEAR, TO ONE WHO, lying on the mound at Ros-na-ree, dreamed in the sunlight, there came an awakening presence, a figure of opalescent radiance who bent over crying. "Can you not see me? Can you not hear me? I come from the Land of Immortal Youth!" This world of Tir-na-nogue, the heaven of the ancient Celt, lay all about them. It lies about us still. Ah, dear land, where the divine ever glimmers brotherly upon us, where the heavens droop nearer in tenderness, and the stones of the field seem more at league with us; what bountiful gifts of wisdom, beauty, and peace dost thou not hold for the world in thy teeming, expanding bosom. O, Eire! There is no dearth in the silence of thy immovable hills, for in their starhearts abide in composed calm the guardians of the paths through which men must go seeking for the immortal waters. Yes, they live, these hills.[13]

You ask me:

    Why do I live

on this green mountain?

  I smile

  No answer

    My heart serene

On flowing water

    peachblow

    quietly going

    far away

  another earth

This is

  another sky

No likeness

  to that human world below

LI PO (699–762), BELOVED POET OF THE T'ANG DYNASTY[14]

Close Encounter

In the course of one of his frequent dialogues with his disciples, someone asked eighth-century Ch'an (Zen) master Hui Hai (known as "The Great Pearl") the following question: "Is Prajñā [transcendent wisdom]* very large?" Here is the exchange that took place:

M: It is.

Q: How large?

M: Unlimited.

Q: Is Prajñā small?

M: It is.

Q: How small?

M: So small as to be invisible.

Q: Where is it?

M: Where is it not?[15]*

---

*The Great Pearl of the T'ang dynasty has described Prajñā as "a substance of absolute purity which contains no single thing on which to lay hold."

In the southwest corner of Saskatchewan not far from Eastend and very near the Montana border, Canadian writer and seeker Sharon Butala apprehends after years of powerful visions and dreams an "absolute, indisputable truth" of the "oneness of the universe." By reason of her spiritual pioneering, Butala begins to recognize the unitive power of the endless prairies.

I LOOKED ACROSS TO THE HILLS on the far side of the valley, shrouded and muted by the fog, and at the closer hills where the mist had dissipated in the sun's rays. I thought of early afternoon during the summer when no animals are stirring, lying deep in their cool burrows or curled up in the shade of a copse of stunted poplars or saskatoons, when even the insects rest under blades of spear grass or cool red stones. Then in the intense, silent heat, hills, stones, burnouts, buffalo grass are imbued with magic, an otherworldly air descends over them.

And what about the end of the day when in the wash of golden light all blemishes fade and disappear and peace descends over the yellow grasses and the luminous sky? Then, too, there is such perfection that all desire for heaven is absorbed in the glowing, fragile plains, the radiant hills.

And in the night, the sky a swirl of glittering stars from its apex an unimaginable distance above, all the way to the precise line of the hills, in the vital darkness of its shadows, the earth has a solidity that is missing from the day. . . .

This morning I bent to smell a yellow clover bloom and a drop of cool, translucent dew touched and clung to the end of my nose. I stood on the bank and looked across the river at the grasses and the yellow and white blooms of cinquefoil and wild aster, at the shiny blue-gray leaves of the wolf willow lining the bank where white-taileds had made trails coming down to water every morning and evening, and where, picking chokecherries, I'd once heard a doe talking to her fawn.

In the purity of the morning, I understand how much more there is to the world than meets the eye, I see that the world fails to dissolve at the edges into myth and dream, only because one wills it not to. . . .[16]

O ancestors, powerful spirits, who live amongst us:

your tombs are the mountains,

your waterfalls are the clouds,

the plants are your jewels.

SUMATRA INCANTATION, INDONESIA[17]

One sod of earth functions as my support; the world and
sky function as my body, sun and moon as my eyes, the
Divine Rabut (very venerable, but not yet definable) is the
real origin of my appearance. . . .

BALINESE RITE IN THE CARE OF THE DEAD[18]

Totem Tree

*I*n 1947 Marco Pallis made a journey into the heart of independent Tibet as it then was and describes that "mysterious presence" embedded in the Tibetan plateau and characteristic of the country's pervasive sacred geography. One becomes conscious, reports Pallis, of "a peculiar quality of transparency affecting the whole atmosphere of the place."[19] He felt himself enveloped by the pellucidity of light, unharnessed and unknowable.

[I]T WAS AS IF THE OBSTACLES TO THE PASSAGE of certain influences had here been thinned down to something quite light and tenuous, obstacles which in the outer world remained dense and opaque. The Himalayan ranges through which one approaches, mounting through their deep-cut gorges, tend to awaken in the mind an ever changing series of vividly separate sense-impressions which in their way are deeply stirring; it would be an insensitive person indeed who did not yield to the magical beauty of slopes all covered with small metallic purple, dark crimson, or white rhododendron from the midst of which blue or yellow Meconopsis poppies raise aloft their crown of flowers; while in damper spots the associated loveliness of dark blue iris and yellow primula seems to offer a foretaste of the delights of *Sukhavati*, the Western Paradise of Amitabha, the Buddha of Light. But once out on the plateau all this is quickly forgotten, for there one finds oneself in a landscape of such ineffable contemplative serenity that all separate impressions coalesce into a single feeling of—how can one best describe it?—yes, of impartiality. It is this quality of the Tibetan landscape which made one call it "transparent," for before all else it preaches the essential emptiness of things and the compassion which is born of an awareness of their vacuity.

If some readers are inclined to dismiss this impression of Tibet as rather fanciful and in any case explainable as an effect, upon an imaginative nature, of a high mountain climate—the valleys are all over 12,000 feet and the air is indescribably exhilarating to both body and mind—this writer can only make answer that though much can reasonably be attributed to such a cause, this is nevertheless insufficient to account in full for the conviction, formed at the time and remaining undimmed after twelve years of absence, that Tibet is a focus of spiritual influence in a particular and objective sense and apart from any power of one's own to respond or otherwise, as the case may be. Essentially, this is a question that pertains to what may properly be called the Science of Sacred Geography, and Tibet is by no means the only example of the kind, though it is one of the most remarkable and extensive.[20]

Camel in Repose

The wise take pleasure in rivers and lakes, the virtuous in mountains; the wise are constantly active, the virtuous still.

CONFUCIUS[21]

$\mathcal{G}$eorge William Russell, who wrote under the pen name AE, experienced the harmonics of the spiritual geography of Ireland from early adolescence. Throughout his life he saw the divine imagination imprinted upon everything "whose whole majesty," he wrote, "is present in the least thing in nature."

THERE IS NO COUNTRY IN THE WORLD whose ancient religion was more inseparably connected with the holy places, mountains, and rivers of the land than Ireland, unless perhaps it be America. We may say it was shaped by the gods. They have left their traces in the streams and lakes which sprung forth at their command. A deity presided over each: their magical tides were fraught with healing powers for they were mixed with elemental fire at their secret sources. . . .

It may be because the land is so full of memorials of an extraordinary past, or it may be that behind the veil these things still endure, but every thing seems possible here. I would feel no surprise if I saw the fiery eyes of the cyclopes wandering over the mountains. There is always a sense expectant of some unveiling about to take place, a feeling, as one wanders at evening down the lanes scented by the honeysuckle, that beings are looking upon us out of the true home of man. While we pace one, isolated in our sad and proud musings, they seem to be saying of us "Soon they will awaken. Soon they will come again to us"; and we pause and look around smitten through by some ancient sweetness, some memory of a life-dawn pure before passion and sin began. The feeling is no less prophetic than reminiscent, and this may account for the unquenchable hope in the future of Ireland which has survived centuries of turbulence, oppression and pain, and which exists in the general heart.

In sleep and dream, in the internal life, a light from that future is thrown upon the spirit which is cheered by it, though unable to phrase to itself the meaning of its own gladness. Perhaps these visions, to which the Celt is so liable, refer as much to the future as to the bygone, and mysteries even more beautiful than the past are yet to be unfolded. I think it is so. There are some to whom a sudden sun-luster from Tir-na-nogue [the heaven of the ancient Celt] revealed a hill on the western shore overlooking the Atlantic. There was a temple with many stately figures: below at the sea's edge jetted twin fountains of the golden fire of life, and far off over a glassy calm of water rose the holy city, the Hy-Brazil [land of immortal youth], in the white sunlight of an inner day.[22]

Oh Mother Earth, Father Sky,

Brother Wind, Friend Light, Sweetheart Water,

Here take my last salutation with folded hands!

For to-day I am melting away into the Supreme

Because my heart became pure,

And all delusion vanished,

Through the power of your good company.

DYING HINDU ASCETIC[23]

Avenue of the Living Stones

essa Bielecki has been called an "apostolic hermit" with a zest for spiritual adventure who is said to embody in many ways the towering and irrepressible spirit of Teresa of Avila. Bielecki's spiritual father, William McNamara, has written that she has "intuited the spirit of St. Teresa. She looks like her, thinks and loves like her, and lives like her." She has recently celebrated her twenty-ninth year as a Carmelite and is the Mother Abbess of two hermitages in Crestone, Colorado, and Kemptville, Nova Scotia. In a short essay entitled "Bridal Mysticism," Bielecki explores the links between the holy mountain of her heart—both real and symbolic—and wayfaring.

THE CARMELITE STORY BEGINS WITH A MOUNTAIN: Mount Carmel, which is located in Palestine, near the modern city of Haifa. I continually delight in the fact that our tradition does not take its name from a person, as do so many other Christian traditions, but from a great chunk of rock. Mount Carmel is rich in history, venerable with age, and the confidante of thousands of stories. It was the scene of numerous Biblical incidents and the home of the prophet Elijah. It was on this mountain that the first Carmelite hermits went to live.

But Mount Carmel is not only geographical and historical; it is also metaphysical and trans-historical. In the *Ascent of Mount Carmel*, for example, John of the Cross outlines the purgative way in terms of climbing this mountain. He describes our path as taking us straight up the face of the mountain; we do not choose the circuitous side paths, which would be easier to travel but would take longer. Carmelites are mountain climbers who go by way of the straight path. Thus Mount Carmel is the homeland of the heart for every Carmelite.

For years I said that it personally didn't matter whether I ever literally saw it or not. But as time has passed I have come to realize that it does matter to me very much. I hope that one day I actually set foot on that holy ground.

Mount Carmel is located in the midst of the desert, and Carmelites are not only mountain climbers; we are also desert rats. The spirituality of the Carmelite tradition is to be equally found in the silence, solitude, and simplicity of the desert. . . .

The first evidence that hermits were living on Mount Carmel dates back to 1155 A.D. Very little is known about these hermits. We don't know whether they were literate or illiterate, whether they were knights or soldiers, clergy or lay people. The important point, very simply, is that they lived on Mount Carmel in the tradition of Elijah and dedicated to Our Lady. The sole purpose of their lives was prayer and contemplation, and their Rule, in a nutshell, was this: We are called to meditate day and night on the law of the Lord, unless engaged in some other just occupation. "Law" in this case does not merely mean the Ten Commandments, but also the law that is written in the universe: the law in our hearts, the natural law, the cosmic law.[24]

*J*ulian Lang always lived close to his grandmother, a storyteller and fluent speaker of the Karuk language that has been spoken for millennia by the people on the upper part of the Klamath River in northwestern California. He is a singer and dancer and a leader in the most important of all Karuk ceremonies, the ceremony to Fix the World, a ritual that contributes to planetary renewal and collective illumination. Lang is also a tribal scholar, Karuk linguist and artist. In this passage from *Ararapikva*, Lang's eloquent translation of four Karuk creation stories, the author sizes up the realms of the holy in Karuk life, which include just about everything.

WE CALL OURSELVES ARAAR, THE PEOPLE. For generation after generation we have been living in our aboriginal homelands located along the Klamath River in northwestern California. Our land is mountainous, heavily wooded, and is the home of deer, bear, mountain lions, Chinook salmon, steelhead and more. It is the land from which we "sprouted up." It teems with thousands of sacred sites, the geographic locations where creation and spiritual events once occurred at the beginning of time. Not so very long ago our people knew every blade of grass, every creek, mountain and ridge. We knew the origin story of every gravel bar, tree species, animal, bird, insect and body of water. . . .

Ikxareeyav means God in the People's language, and refers both to our many spirit-deities, and nowadays, to the monotheistic God of modern religions. We have deified everything in the natural world. We consider all of nature to be alive, possessing both feeling and a consciousness. Hence the *natural world* is capable of seeing and hearing us, "blessing" us, and taking pity on us. The Earth is a physical manifestation of God's creative spirit, and we, Human Beings, are recognized by the Earth as a part of the natural world. Once I asked my one hundred and eleven year old great-grandmother, Bessie Tripp, "Who did the old Indians say was God, Grandma?" She said, "Why, the Earth! Ever'thin.' The rocks, the leaves, the mountains." Our sense is that all of nature grows from the Earth as strands of long hair connecting the present with the beginning of time and original knowledge.

Our wisdom tells us that the *Ikxareeyavs* lived on this world before Human Beings. They grew on this earth-world (as we subsequently were to grow as well). The *Ikxareeyavs* were hyper-alive, meaning their lives were purely creative. Each moment of their existence resulted in some kind of creation: the realization of a natural law, a powerful song, or a healing herb and medicine formula to cure the gravest ill. The Earth itself was new when they were alive. And, like a new love, every moment, every movement, every idea and feeling was without precedent.

All of the natural world from the earthworm to the mammals, trees, specific geological formations (certain granite outcroppings, for example), sacred sites, mountains, creeks, the sun, the moon, even the mosquito, were once *Ikxareeyav* People. Each *Ikxareeyav* experienced an intense and emotional existence. For example, a despised and ill-born man escaped his own murder and was transformed into the moon. Our little sacred mountain, Sugar Loaf (*A'uuyich*), was once an *Ikxareeyav* Spirit-man who, being motivated by love, invented all the fishing and hunting tools, and much of our dance regalia. In fact, Sugar Loaf's creative powers resulted in much of what anthropologists call our "material culture." The impressive falls on the Klamath River located at *Ka'tim'iin* (Somes Bar) were created by an enraged

Ikxareeyav woman many years ago. Wherever our ancestors looked or walked in the Karuk world, there was an *Ikxareeyav* associated with the place. . . .

It is easy to overlook the sacredness of land nowadays, but it's as foolish today as it would have been 150 years ago. It's encouraging to know that our *Ikxareeyavs* rarely recede into oblivion. After all, are there not yet rattlesnakes? Or frogs, eels, mountains, creeks, trees, and sacred ceremonies? If you look closely enough you'll see they are all *Ikxareeyavs*.[25]

*W*hat sets monks apart from the rest of us is not an overbearing piety but a contemplative sense of fun," writes the poet, author, and Benedictine oblate Kathleen Norris in her mirthful, meditative evocation of the Great Plains and its far-reaching sway over the human spirit. From Lemmon, South Dakota, Norris reports on the spiritual geography of a grandly idiosyncratic universe that is at once mythic, contradictory, sublime, desolate, prayerful, and full of hope.

THE SILENCE OF THE PLAINS, this great unpeopled landscape of earth and sky, is much like the silence one finds in a monastery, an unfathomable silence that has the power to re-form you. And the Plains have changed me. . . .

I am not a monk, although I have a formal relationship with the Benedictines as an oblate, or associate, of a community of some sixty-five monks. As a married woman, thoroughly Protestant, who often has more doubt than anything resembling faith, this surprises me almost as much as finding that the Great Plains themselves have become my monastery, my place set apart, where I thrive and grow. . . .

It was the Plains that first drew me to the monastery, which I suppose is ironic, for who would go seeking a desert within a desert? Both Plains and monastery are places where distractions are at a minimum and you must rely on your own resources, only to find yourself utterly dependent on forces beyond your control; where time seems to stand still, as it does in the liturgy; where your life is defined by waiting. . . .

The deprivations of Plains life and monastic life tend to turn small gifts into treasures, and gratitude is one of the first flowers to spring forth when hope is rewarded and the desert blooms. When the drought broke and gave us the wettest spring I've witnessed in eighteen years on the Plains, the exultant greenness of the land was enough to make people weep for joy. "Take a look," one rancher said, "you may not see it like this again in your lifetime." The most pessimistic among us were reduced to muttering, "it won't last." We know it won't last, not in Dakota, and we stay anyway. That is our glory, both folly and strength.[26]

Boscawen-un Stone Circle (triptych)

$\mathcal{W}$riting from Bangkok in 1971, British scholar and Buddhist John Blofeld (1913–1987) comments in the preface to his spiritual autobiography, *The Wheel of Life*, that his initiation experience on the summit of Tashiding in the 1950s continued to be the highlight of his life. In his lifelong quest for wisdom and truth, Blofeld exhibited a self-deprecating wit and disarming candor that is both unusual and inviting in that it comes from a distinguished mind dedicated to the pursuit of the One. His colorful and humorous descriptions of the ludicrousness of his own foibles, not to mention those of others, suggest a playfully aware spirit. He reported that his caravan "could have inspired illustrations for a Chinese translation of *Canterbury Tales*." He found "the motion of my wheel-less vehicle [a cross between a sedan-chair and the cabin of a very small boat slung between two mules walking in single file] so soothing that I passed much of the time stretched flat on my back, dozing or drowsily busy with my thoughts, except now and then when I remembered that this was a pilgrimage and shamed myself into sitting cross-legged for an hour, practising meditation. More genuine pilgrims felt obliged to go on foot; indeed, Mongols often make far longer journeys, crawling on their knees or stopping at every three paces to prostrate themselves. . . ."[27]

Blofeld experienced Chinese Buddhism and Taoism at a critical historical juncture—just moments before it was subsumed by Communist rule. His years in Peking and his travels throughout China, Mongolia, India, Burma, and Tibet in search of self-knowledge placed him on a genuine spiritual path that challenged him throughout his life: "Often I have longed for the Light, but not ardently enough to carry me beyond all lesser pursuits,"[28] he wrote characteristically of the pitfalls of his journey to the mountaintop. His reflections on the power of place to metamorphose consciousness reveal the pilgrim soul of an inspiring seeker.

THE POWER-DRENCHED BEAUTY OF THE DAWN at Tashiding in Sikkim—that glittering spectacle of fire dancing across ice—it must seem to the weariest traveller a lavish reward for the discomforts of two days' journey through waterlogged and leech-infested jungles. But to me it was more than this. It had come to hold an inner significance, impossible not to sense, but very hard to describe. I even thought of it as a kind of spiritual baptism, a miraculous soothing of body and mind, to be daily renewed for as long as I remained upon the sacred mountain. Twice already it had made me vitally aware of the dormant forces which, so my Teachers insist, lie hidden and generally quite unsuspected within every man's deepest consciousness. I had even sensed that the fantastic metamorphosis of snow into multi-coloured fire so fittingly accompanied by the unearthly music of the place, magically reflected a meaning beyond all meanings, the ultimate Goal which had until now always seemed impossibly far away. Might not fragments of my mind, shattered like thin glass by the glitter and thunderous noise, suddenly undergo a kaleidoscopic change, and falling into place, reveal that state of pure serenity which lies beyond the highest levels of conceptual thought? Might not the moment have arrived for me to grasp that which the [Chinese] sage Huang Po so profoundly terms the Ungraspable? Each morning at dawn, for just as long as the colours danced before me, nothing in the realm of mystical experience seemed wholly beyond my reach.[29]

Those of us who live beneath this cold mountain

have heard its voice in our dreams, felt its arms

lift us out of warm rooms and soft beds, up

onto its shoulders where we are light as leaves.

Amy Barratt, Canadian poet,

"The Mountain"[30]

A venerated European teacher and writer (of Andean and Bolivian ancestry), Lama Anagarika Govinda (1898–1985) spent a large part of his life studying at the feet of Tibetan masters. His early years in Italy and Germany were influenced by his membership in the Buddhist communities that flourished there in the 1920s. He lived in Ceylon, Burma, Sikkim, India, and Tibet as pilgrim, painter, hermit, and student. Later on he traveled the world as a Buddhist scholar and interpreter.

In the spring of 1933 Lama Govinda journeyed to the Chang-Thang, the vast northern highlands of Tibet where "the gates of heaven were opened" and a revolving world of fantastic shapes, forms, and colors revealed itself with such suddenness that "one began to doubt their reality as well as one's own." Lama Govinda often referred to his pilgrimages to the sacred land of Tibet as "the great miracle." He came to know Tibet as a state of mind where the universe was no mere abstraction but "a matter of direct experience" of infinite depths regulated only by the celestial bodies. In *The Way of the White Clouds*, Lama Govinda explores his lifelong relationship to the holy ground and realm that is called "the land of the thousand Buddhas."

THE GREAT RHYTHM OF NATURE pervades everything, and man is woven into it with mind and body. Even his imagination does not belong so much to the realm of the individual as to the soul of the landscape, in which the rhythm of the universe is condensed into a melody of irresistible charm. Imagination here becomes an adequate expression of reality on the plane of human consciousness, and this consciousness seems to communicate itself from individual to individual till it forms a spiritual atmosphere that envelops the whole of Tibet.

Thus a strange transformation takes place under the influence of this country, in which the valleys are as high as the highest peaks of Europe and where mountains soar into space beyond the reach of humans. It is as if a weight were lifted from one's mind, or as if certain hindrances were removed. Thoughts flow easily and spontaneously without losing their direction and coherence, a high degree of concentration and clarity is attained almost without effort and a feeling of elevated joy keeps one's mind in a creative mood. Consciousness seems to be raised to a higher level, where the obstacles and disturbances of ordinary life do not exist, except as a faint memory of things which have lost all their importance and attraction. At the same time one becomes more sensitive and open to new forms of reality; the intuitive qualities of our mind are awakened and stimulated—in short, there are all the conditions for attaining the higher stages of meditation or *dhyana*.[31]

Giraffe Detail

*O*ne of the most important places on earth for eighty-two-year-old geologist, scholar, Passionist priest, and far-seeing ecological thinker Thomas Berry is an obscure little meadow in the Appalachians. He discovered it as a young boy, and as the years passed he realized that it served as a model of hope and inspiration for his passionate engagement in the re-memberment of the world about us. Nature revealed to Berry the numinous underpinnings of life itself—though he did not know that at the time—and over the next seven decades that early experience of the meadowland informed and directed his thoughts.

I WAS A YOUNG PERSON THEN, some ten years old. My family was moving from a more settled part of a southern town out to the edge of town where the new house was being built. The house, not yet finished, was situated on a slight incline. Down below was a small creek and there across the creek was a meadow. It was an early afternoon in May when I first looked down over the scene and saw the meadow. The field was covered with lilies rising above the thick grass. A magic moment, this experience gave to my life something, I know not what, that seems to explain my life at a more profound level than almost any other experience that I can remember.

It was not only the lilies. It was the singing of the crickets and the woodlands in the distance and the clouds in a clear sky. It was not something conscious that happened just then. I went on about my life as any young person might do. Perhaps it was not simply this moment that made such a deep impression upon me. Perhaps it was a sensitivity that was developed throughout my childhood. Yet as the years pass this moment returns to me and whenever I think about my basic life attitude and the whole trend of my mind and causes that I have given my efforts to I seem to come back to this moment and the impact it has had on my feeling for what is real and worthwhile in life.

This early experience, it seems, has become normative for me throughout the entire range of my thinking. Whatever preserves and enhances this meadow in the natural cycles of its transformation is good, what is opposed to this meadow or negates it is not good. My life orientation is that simple. It is also that pervasive. It applies in economics and political orientation as well as in education and religion and whatever. . . .

The more a person thinks of the infinite number of interrelated activities that take place here the more mysterious it all becomes, the more meaning a person finds in the Maytime blooming of the lilies, the more awestruck a person might be in simply looking out over this little patch of meadowland. It had none of the majesty of the Appalachian or western mountains, none of the immensity or the power of the oceans, nor even the harsh magnificence of desert country; yet in this little meadow the deep mystery of existence is manifested in a manner as profound and as impressive as any other place that I have known in these past many years.[32]

Canine Dream

. . . the views of nature held by any people determine all their institutions.

RALPH WALDO EMERSON, *ENGLISH TRAITS*[33]

If nature is your teacher, your soul will awaken.

GOETHE'S *FAUST*[34]

THE CATHEDRALS WITHIN

Our real journey in life is interior; it is a matter of growth, deepening,
and of an ever greater surrender to the creative action of love and grace
in our hearts. Never was it more necessary for us to respond to that action.

THOMAS MERTON (1915–1968), TRAPPIST MONK,
POET, AND WRITER[1]

All we are is in the soul.

HONORÉ DE BALZAC (1799–1850)[2]

Tree Knees

*H*ildegard of Bingen, the great twelfth-century Rhineland visionary, theologian, musician, artist, preacher, and writer, credits her soul as the spiritual locus of her sacred journey wherein her consciousness is set free to roam the deepest layers of the unconscious. Hildegard expresses her central vision (she had many) as the profound attainment of a oneness remembered accompanied by a liberating experience of unconditional love.

SINCE MY CHILDHOOD, I have always seen a light in my soul, but not with the outer eyes, nor through the thoughts of my heart; neither do the five outer senses take part in this vision. . . . The light I perceive is not of a local kind, but is much brighter than the cloud which bears the sun. I cannot distinguish height, breadth, or length in it. . . . What I see or learn in such a vision stays long in my memory. I see, hear, and know in the same moment. . . . I cannot recognize any sort of form in this light, although I sometimes see in it another light that is known to me as the living light. . . . While I am enjoying the spectacle of this light, all sadness and sorrow vanish from my memory. . . . [3]

*I*n a conversation with Albert Einstein on the nature of reality in July 1930 at Einstein's residence in Kaputh, Germany, Rabindranath Tagore described the roots of his own spiritual aspirations: "My religion is in the reconciliation of the Super-personal Man, the Universal human spirit, in my own individual being."[4] To this end, he founded an experimental school in Santiniketan ("abode of peace"), about one hundred miles from Calcutta, which mushroomed in his lifetime into a great center of culture and education that came to be known as Visva-Bharati ("world university"). High on the curriculum was the inspiration and experience of Nature as divine teacher. His own encounters with the numinous in the natural world doubtless contributed to his unique concepts of creative education. Tagore relates an early experience of cosmic consciousness that was triggered by a few Bengali words heavily freighted with the essence of nature.

I HAD A DEEP SENSE, almost from infancy, of nature, a feeling of intimate companionship with the trees and the clouds, and the touch of season. At the same time I had a peculiar susceptibility to human kindness. . . .

I remember the day in my childhood when, after the painful process of learning my Bengali alphabet, I unexpectedly came to the first simple combination of letters which gave me the words: "It rains, the leaves tremble." I was thrilled with the picture which these words suggested to me. The fragments lost their individual isolation and my mind revelled in the unity of a vision. In a similar manner, on that morning in the village, the facts of my life suddenly appeared to me in a luminous unity. All things that had seemed like vagrant waves were revealed in relation to a boundless sea, and from that time I have been able to maintain the faith that, in all my experience of nature or man, there is the fundamental truth of spiritual reality.[5]

Three Graces

If you rip open my heart, Holy Father, you will find there only dances and tales—nothing else. . . . Shall I continue, Holy Father?

I am listening.

When an almond tree became covered with blossoms in the heart of winter, all the trees around it began to jeer. "What vanity," they screamed, "what insolence! Just think, it believes it can bring spring in this way!" The flowers of the almond tree blushed with shame. "Forgive me, my sisters," said the tree. "I swear I did not want to blossom, but suddenly I felt a warm springtime breeze in my heart."

NIKOS KAZANTZAKIS (1883–1957), *SAINT FRANCIS*[6]

*T*ertullian, a renowned Christian writer of the late second and early third centuries, lived in the ancient city of Carthage in North Africa. His writings greatly influenced Western theology. The language and character of the soul were of particular interest to the visionary theologian. In *De Testimonio Animae* (*On the Testimony of the Soul*), Tertullian points to the unassailable realities of the soul that are grounded in the numinosity of Nature and inseparable from it. A cardinal aspect of Tertullian's soul is the splendor of the human spirit, "an illumination thrown upon life," to cite a locution once used to describe the spirit of Balzac.

THESE TESTIMONIES OF THE SOUL are as simple as they are true, as obvious as they are simple, as common as they are obvious, as natural as they are common, as divine as they are natural. I think that they cannot appear to any one to be trifling and ridiculous if he considers the majesty of Nature, whence the authority of the soul is derived. What you allow to the mistress you will assign to the disciple. Nature is the mistress, the soul is the disciple; what the one has taught, or the other has learned, has been delivered to them by God, who is, in truth, the Master even of the mistress herself. What notion the soul is able to conceive of her first teacher is in your power to judge, from that soul which is in you. Feel that which causes you to feel; think upon that which is in forebodings your prophet; in omens, your augur; in the events which befall you, your foreseer. Strange if, being given by God, she knows how to act the diviner for men! Equally strange if she knows Him by whom she has been given![7]

Treebeard

*D*arwin, the agnostic, and Melville, the Presbyterian, reveal contrasting visions of a pervasive, transcendent presence at large in the universe, derived from their close observations of the natural world, while mutually engaged in the inquiry of Self.

DARWIN:

THE FEELING OF RELIGIOUS DEVOTION is a highly complex one, consisting of love, complete submission to an exalted and mysterious superior, a strong sense of dependence, fear, reverence, gratitude, hope for the future, and perhaps other elements. No being could experience so complex an emotion until advanced in his intellectual and moral faculties to at least a moderately high level. Nevertheless, we see some distant approach to this state of mind in the deep love of a dog for his master, associated with complete submission, some fear, and perhaps other feelings.

MELVILLE:

HOW NOBLY IT RISES our conceit of the mighty, misty monster, to behold him solemnly sailing through a calm tropical sea; his vast, mild head overhung by a canopy of vapor, engendered by his incom-municable contemplations, and that vapor—as you will sometimes see it—glorified by a rainbow, as if Heaven itself had put its seal upon his thoughts. For, d'ye see, rainbows do not visit the clear air; they only irradiate vapor. And so, through all the thick mists of the dim doubts in my mind, divine intuitions now and then shoot, enkindling my fog with a heavenly ray. And for this I thank God; for all have doubts; many deny; but doubts or denials, few along with them, have intuitions. Doubts of all things earthly, and intuitions of some things heavenly; this combination makes neither believer nor infidel, but makes a man who regards them both with equal eye.[8]

$\mathcal{C}$anadian playwright and novelist Blanche Howard begins her unusual, whimsical, fantastical short story, "A Good Day on a Minor Galaxy," with an epigraph by Joseph Campbell: "This body is a vehicle of consciousness." Howard maneuvers this turn of thought into a launching pad for a modern minimyth in which she posits a series of planetwide miraculous events attributable to "a five-minute burst of heightened consciousness on the planet Earth" with peculiar consequences. Repercussions range from eyewitness accounts of "tears falling from the stone eyes of the Virgin Mary at Lourdes" to thousands in India "dazzled by a vision of jasmine sprouting from the Buddha's navel." The full sweep of Howard's playful insights into "the eye of the soul" (in the words of Blake), can only be appreciated in their entirety. Nonetheless, the following passage does convey her knack for turning spiritual ecstasy on its head, then planting it in common ground.

IT WAS FIVE O'CLOCK IN THE AFTERNOON, the time of the day when Mme. Truffault watered the *jardin* behind her stone house in the village of Legna (permanent population fifty) in the Jura mountains of France. Today's meagre offering, unfortunately, scarcely stained the earth, for the dry and cracked soil was thirsty beyond the possibilities of Madame's battered watering can. She sighed and bent to pinch a dead leaf from a geranium, then rested her eyes for encouragement on its single crimson flower.

As she did so, the colour seemed, suddenly, to flare outward like the flame of a candle when wax is dropped into it. Hesitating, she drew her hand back. Before her wondering eyes the unlikely illumination intensified until crimson began to leak from the flower in small banners of colour, curling outwards in hesitant tendrils, venturing further and further, seeping into the cracks in the earth, and finally vibrating in a dizzying borealis around the geranium core.

As the crimson began to intrude into the pores and interstices of a body unused to housing even temporal delight, Mme. Truffault was surprised by pleasure—an emotion now infrequently encountered, but dimly remembered in association with girlhood and a field of poppies. Then mere pleasure slipped away and she was wracked and lifted up by something akin to exultation.

She dropped the watering can and straightened, holding her arms to the sky. Crimson flares emerged from her fingertips, powerful streams of light that could ignite the world. She stood, sending flames into the blue for what seemed an eternity, but was in reality only five minutes. At the end of that time the colour began to retreat, from her fingertips, from her body, then from the earth, and finally settled itself into the everyday crimson of its rightful owner.

Mme. Truffault gathered up her gardening tools, and after supper she went to late mass, where she thanked the Blessed Virgin for exalting her for a little while into a state of grace. At the end of her prayer she whispered and truly believed, that she was now ready for Heaven, whenever it should be God's will.

She did not mention the incident to M. Truffault—M. Truffault was not on good terms with the Virgin Mary—since she wanted to nourish the memory in the privacy of her soul, where he couldn't get at it.[9]

Pregnant Wolf Howling

$\mathcal{H}$adewijch II, a thirteenth-century Flemish Beguine—a member of the movement of laywomen who created independent spiritual communities throughout northern Europe—describes the unitive source that perpetuates and illumines existence.

You who want knowledge,
seek the Oneness
within
There you will find
the clear mirror
already waiting.[10]

*D*o you wish to hear the temple bells?" asks Jesuit scholar Anthony de Mello. If so, then "listen to the sound of the sea," he advises. De Mello relates a parable that suggests the infinite messages of creation.

THE TEMPLE WAS BUILT on an island and it held a thousand bells. Big bells, small bells, bells fashioned by the finest craftsmen in the world. When a wind blew or a storm raged, all the bells would peal out in unison, a symphony that would send the heart of the hearer into raptures.

But over the centuries the island sank into the sea and, with it, the temple bells. An ancient legend said that the bells continued to peal out, ceaselessly, and could be heard by anyone who listened attentively. Inspired by this tradition, a young man travelled thousands of miles, determined to hear those bells. He sat for days on the shore, facing the vanished island, and listened with all his might. But all he could hear was the sound of the sea. He made every effort to push away the sound of the waves so that he could hear the bells. But to no avail; the sound of the sea seemed to flood the world.

He kept at his task for weeks. When he got disheartened he would listen to the words of the village pundits who spoke with unction of the legend of the temple bells and of those who had heard them and proved the legend to be true. Then his heart would be aflame as he heard their words . . . only to become discouraged again when weeks of further effort yielded no results.

Finally he decided to give up the attempt. Perhaps he was not destined to hear the bells. Perhaps the legend was not true. It was his final day, and he went to the shore to say goodbye to the sea and the sky and the wind and the coconut trees. He lay on the sands, and for the first time listened to the sound of the sea. He did not resist that sound that day. Soon he was so lost in the sound that he was barely conscious of himself, so deep was the silence that the sound produced.

In the depth of that silence, he heard it! The tinkle of a tiny bell followed by another, and another and another . . . and soon every one of the thousand temple bells was pealing out in harmony, and his heart was rapt in joyous ecstasy.[11]

*M*ore than 334 million people on the planet call themselves Buddhists. Their inspiration derives from a sixth-century B.C. princely seer, Siddhartha Gautama (ca. 566–ca. 486 B.C.), who traveled and sought his own self-realization assiduously and whose influence has been profound for more than twenty-five hundred years. Called Buddha, the Sanskrit/Pali word for "one who has awakened" and "one who knows," Siddhartha is the founder of Buddhism. Summoned by the venerable fig tree, Siddhartha receives illumination. Buddhist, teacher, and writer Stephanie Kaza interprets the Buddha's quest for cosmic knowledge.

WHEN THE BUDDHA ARRIVED at Bodh Gaya [the most sacred place on earth for Buddhists, in northeast India; where Buddha attained enlightenment], he had been on a long journey in search of the truth. Wise men, hermits, and ascetics had offered him their teachings, but he was not satisfied. Though he had disciplined his body to the point of starvation and challenged his mind to the edge of its limits, he still had not found the deepest truth of existence. His determination burned in him like a steady flame; with all his heart he wanted to penetrate the way to true understanding.

In his passion and yearning, he was called by a large fig tree to sit at its feet. This was the destination of his pilgrimage; he had come with his empty body and mind to receive great wisdom. He vowed to not move from the tree until he found the Great Truth. For seven days and seven nights he sat in meditation, supported by the tree. During the seventh night he was tormented by every possible distraction of the mind. Mara, the voice of delusion, challenged him ferociously, asking what right he had to sit by the fig tree seeking the truth. To counter the force of ignorance, he touched his right hand to the earth. With the earth and tree as witness, the powerful realization of interdependence was revealed.[12]

Yoda

Better to know oneself, said an early monk, than to work miracles.

As recounted by
Dom Laurence Freeman, O. S. B.[13]

Abū Yazīd of Bistam, a ninth-century Islamic mystic, describes the ascent of his spirit to the heavens of the eternal Self.

THEN I BECAME AS A BIRD, whose body was of Oneness and whose wings were of Everlastingness, and I continued to fly in the air of the Absolute, until I passed into the sphere of Purification, and gazed upon the field of Eternity, and beheld there the Tree of Oneness. When I looked I myself was all those.[14]

*O*n a journey to Israel in 1976, novelist Saul Bellow describes an *aperçu* he had in Jerusalem in which the spirit of the universe reveals itself and in turn becomes a reflection of Bellow himself. "We step into the street," he writes,

AND MY FRIEND . . . takes a deep breath and advises me to do the same. The air, the air itself, is thought-nourishing in Jerusalem, the Sages themselves said so. I am prepared to believe it. I know that it must have special properties. The delicacy of the light also affects me. I look downward toward the Dead Sea, over broken rocks and small houses with bulbous roofs. The color of these is that of the ground itself, and on this strange deadness the melting air presses with an almost human weight. Something intelligible, something metaphysical is communicated by these colors. The universe interprets itself before your eyes in the openness of the rock-jumbled valley ending in dead water. Elsewhere you die and disintegrate. Here you die and mingle. . . . This atmosphere makes the American commonplace "out of this world" true enough to give your soul a start.[15]

*A*uthor Thomas Buckley tells a story about his revered teacher—an uncle who had been apprenticed to a Yurok Indian "high man" on the Klamath River. Buckley admired his uncle's equanimity, an imperturbability that endured even though all that the older man had cherished was gone—the elders, the old ways, and the great ancient trees. His uncle invariably perceived the world under the guise of the eternal: "Light," he would say, is "the normal course of events." At a time when Buckley's own life was in profound disarray, his uncle took him on a trip deep into the coastal mountains of California, a place the author had often heard about and which he understood to be a site of power and knowledge. During the trip, to his great astonishment, he experienced a shift in consciousness—mystical in its intensity—in which he was introduced to his own divinity.

[A]S I WALKED I SAW that it was not the same trail at all. Each outcropping of pinkish basaltic shist, each Brewer's spruce, western hemlock, yellow pine, each blade of grass, thimbleberry, blackberry, red huckleberry, each snow plant, bracken fern, angelica leaf and vine maple, small dragonfly, nuthatch and bandtailed pigeon, fallen white cedar and dried shelf fungus, wrinkle and crack on the fungus, ripple in the stream and pebble in the trail, each was purely itself, just light, distinct from all else and also completely at home in a single, multiform place of dazzling complexity and beauty. Oddly, the more distinctly etched and beautiful the earth became the more transparent it was, as though it were only the lid on the cauldron of the world. And that lid shifted aside so that I was seeing into the kettle itself and finding it probably bottomless, bubbling with layers and layers of beings and things unimagined and, even then, seeing it clearly, still unimaginable (even as fantastic creatures), probably never to be fully grasped, although I knew there were those who had gone far in this.

The sun was bright through the trees, the air filling me with its clarity, dissolving me into light, the light and the air breathed becoming a single field of being in which I flowed, anonymously, joining the ranks of myriads of beings that are the uniquely manifested forms of that field, coming and going on mysterious yet perfectly ordered and perfectly compassionate rounds, coming and going in beauty. And as, when I'd seen each thing on the surface of the world as utterly distinct, perfectly formed and autonomous, then that surface had knit into a single, whole, and unblemished fabric, so now, finding myself nameless and of no particular strength or merit in an eternal succession of things and beings seen and unseen, benign, innocuous, and highly dangerous, I became more and more distinct to myself, each breath and footfall, the weight of my body and light of my eye as real as the song that rode then in the stirring of the air.[16]

Utah Pharaoh

O Servant, where dost thou seek Me?

Lo! I am beside thee.

I am neither in the temple nor in the mosque:

    I am neither in Kaaba nor in Kailash:

Neither am I in rites and ceremonies,

    nor in Yoga and renunciation.

If thou art a true seeker, thou shalt at once see Me.

Thou shalt meet me in a moment's time.

KABIR (1440–1518), POET, SAGE,

SAINT-SINGER OF BENARES, NORTH INDIA[17]

In his classic work, *Tristes Tropiques*, Claude Lévi-Strauss sets forth his quest for "a human society reduced to its most basic expression." His journey from central Brazil to southern Asia takes on, at times, the shades of a spiritual safari as he records events, such as this one—a recognition of mutual human need and yearning.

I REMEMBER A WALK along Clifton Beach, which is on the Indian Ocean near Karachi. After two miles of dunes and marshes, you come to a long beach of dark sand. On that particular day it was deserted, but on feast days crowds make their way there in carriages drawn by camels even more garishly bedecked than their masters. The ocean was a greenish white, and the sun was setting; all illumination seemed to be rising from the sand and the sea, while the sky above appeared to be set against the light. An old man, in a turban, had fashioned a small mosque for himself with the help of two iron chairs borrowed from a neighbouring eating-house, where kebabs were roasting. He was all alone on the beach, and he was praying.[18]

*T*he Third Patriarch of Zen, seventh-century Chinese master Seng Ts'an, one of twenty-eight patriarchs, who were considered to be the direct transmitters of the ortho-dox line of Buddhism, advises:

> WHEN THE TEN THOUSAND THINGS are viewed in their
>   oneness,
> We return to the origin and remain where we have always
>   been. . . .
> One in all,
> All in One—
> If only this is realized,
> No more worry about not being perfect![19]

Ch'ing, the chief carpenter, was carving wood into a stand for musical instruments. When finished, the work appeared to those who saw it as though of supernatural execution; and the Prince of Lu asked him, saying, "What mystery is there in your art?"

"No mystery, Your Highness," replied Ch'ing. "And yet there is something. When I am about to make such a stand, I guard against any diminution of my vital power. I first reduce my mind to absolute quiescence. Three days in this condition, and I become oblivious of any reward to be gained. Five days, and I become oblivious of any fame to be acquired. Seven days, and I become unconscious of my four limbs and my physical frame. Then, with no thought of the Court present in my mind, my skill becomes concentrated, and all disturbing elements from without are gone. I enter some mountain forest, I search for a suitable tree. It contains the form required, which is afterwards elaborated. I see the stand in my mind's eye, and then set to work. Beyond that there is nothing. I bring my own native capacity into relation with that of the wood. What was suspected to be of supernatural execution in my work was due solely to this.

CHUANG TZU (CA. 399–295 B.C.), CHINESE SAGE[20]

Tasmanian writer Howard Murphet began visiting India in 1964 to study yoga and Eastern philosophy. Earlier, he served with the British Eighth Army from El Alamein to Tunis and also participated in the D day invasion of Normandy. In his 1993 book, *Where the Road Ends*, he describes the opening of his spiritual heart center while sitting one morning under the great banyan tree at Adyar, near Madras in South India.

THE GROUND UNDER THE GREAT SPREADING TREE was covered with sand and the many trunks coming down to the ground gave it the appearance of a natural cathedral. Occasionally, lectures were given under this tree, but on this sunny morning I sat alone there, in the leafy shade, looking through the slender columns that held up the green canopy of its roof. There seemed to be an otherworldly spiritual beauty about it. Suddenly, without warning, I was sitting in the *jyothi*, the divine Light. It was all around me and within me. The physical world did not entirely disappear but seemed as if it had been pushed over to one side, some distance away, but the whole natural cathedral of the banyan tree disappeared and was replaced by the divine Light. The sunlight, that I could still discern in the world outside, seemed as weak as candlelight in comparison to the brightness, splendour and glory of the true divine Light. Yet the brightness did not hurt my eyes. It seemed to soothe them. Perhaps I was not seeing it by my natural eyes but by an inner sight of the spirit. The experience, with the inexpressible ecstasy that it brought, did not last long. I knew it had come as a gift of reassurance and encouragement from God and I thanked him.[21]

A maverick in his use of typography, New England poet e. e. cummings (1894–1962) was also a linguistic radical. His experimentation with punctuation, fracturing of words, and the use of verbs as nouns gave his poetry an unusual appearance that has invigorated and enriched our language. Although the following selected lines from "i am a little church" display little of cummings's innovative visual appeal," they do reflect a spirit in communion with the mystery of life from a poet who once said: "We can never be born enough. We are human beings;for whom is birth is a supremely welcome mystery,the mystery of growing:the mystery which happens only and whenever we are faithful to ourselves."

> i am a little church(no great cathedral)
> far from the splendor and squalor of hurrying cities. . . .
>
> around me surges a miracle of unceasing
> birth and glory and death and resurrection:
> over my sleeping self float flaming symbols
> of hope,and i wake to a perfect patience of mountains
>
> i am a little church(far from the frantic
> world with its rapture and anguish)at peace with nature. . . .
>
> winter by spring,i lift my diminutive spire to
> merciful Him Whose only now is forever. . . .[22]

Mating Ritual

The Bauls of Bengal are bards from northeastern India. The word *baul* means "mad" and refers to the peripatetic minstrels who eschew conventional Hinduism and Islam. Deeply influenced by Sufi mysticism, the Bauls greatly affected seventeenth- and eighteenth-century Bengali writing. One of their songs, nearly two centuries old, exalts the eternal realm where love is ultimate—the sacred abode of the Supreme Spirit.

IT GOES ON BLOSSOMING FOR AGES, the soul-lotus, in which I am bound, as well as thou, without escape. There is no end to the opening of its petals, and the honey in it has so much sweetness that thou, like an enchanted bee, canst never desert it, and therefore thou art bound, and I am, and *mukti* [liberation of the soul] is nowhere.[23]

As the sheath

and branching leaves

of the plantain

are seen in its stem,

so You are the stem

of the universe

and all is visible

in You.

Hindu prayer to Vishnu, the Preserver[24]

𝒮aint Gregory of Nyssa (ca. 335–ca. 395), a principal interpreter and architect of the ascetic and mystical tradition of Eastern monasticism, describes the Eternal One's "unknowability" by the human mind and declares that the fullness of creation is altogether ineffable and incomprehensible.

IT IS LIKE A PERPENDICULAR CLIFF of smooth rock, rearing up from the limitless expanse of sea to its top that overhangs the sheer abyss. Imagine what a man feels when he stands right on the edge, and sees that there is no hold for hand or foot: the mind feels in just the same way when, in its quest for the Nature that is outside time and space, it finds that all footholds have been left behind. There is nothing to "take hold of," neither place nor time nor dimension nor anything else, nothing on which thought can take its stand. At every turn the mind feels the ungraspable escape its grasp, it becomes giddy, there is no way out.[25]

Cliff Faces

Two students from the University of Paris came to visit John Ruysbroeck, the great medieval mystic of Flanders (1293–1381), and asked him to furnish them with a short phrase or motto that might serve them as a rule of life.

Vos estis tam sancti sicut vultis, Ruysbroeck answered.

"You are as holy as you will to be."[26]

*F*ive years after entering the Abbey of Our Lady of Gethsemani, a Trappist monastery in a valley near Louisville, Kentucky, Thomas Merton began a journal that recorded the transformations that take place in the depths of a monk's soul. These interior developments often coincided with the profound "sacramental" moments of life as well as the rudiments of daily monastic labors. Merton also experienced that the life of a soul advances regardless of such influences. Near the completion of his turn on the fire watch of Gethsemani one hot summer's night in July 1952, Merton climbs the shaking twisted staircase to the ancient bells and bursts into dialogue with Spirit.

AND NOW MY WHOLE BEING breathes the wind which blows through the belfry, and my hand is on the door through which I see the heavens. The door swings out upon a vast sea of darkness and of prayer. Will it come like this, the moment of my death? Will You open a door upon the great forest and set my feet upon a ladder under the moon, and take me out among the stars?

The roof glistens under my feet, this long metal roof facing the forest and the hills, where I stand higher than the treetops and walk upon shining air.

Mists of damp heat rise up out of the fields around the sleeping abbey. The whole valley is flooded with moonlight and I can count the southern hills beyond the watertank, and almost number the trees of the forest to the north. Now the huge chorus of living beings rises up out of the world beneath my feet: life singing in the watercourses, throbbing in the creeks and the fields and the trees, choirs of millions and millions of jumping and flying and creeping things. And far above me the cool sky opens upon the frozen distance of the stars.

I lay the clock upon the belfry ledge and pray cross-legged with my back against the tower, and face the same unanswered question.

Lord God of this great night: do You see the woods? Do You hear the rumor of their loneliness? Do You behold their secrecy? Do You remember their solitudes? Do You see that my soul is beginning to dissolve like wax within me?[27]

$\mathcal{S}$aint Seraphim of Sarov (1759–1883) is a beloved popular saint in Russia. In his famous "Conversation" with his disciple Motovilov, Saint Seraphim reveals the nature of mystical union with the divine.

As they sit together in the snowy woods of Sarov, Motovilov experiences his spiritual father's state of transcendence through a light made visible:

PICTURE IN THE SUN'S ORB, in the most dazzling brightness of its noon-day shining, the face of a man who is talking to you. You can see his lips moving, the expression in his eyes, you hear his voice, you feel his arms round your shoulders, and yet you see neither his arms, nor his body, nor his face, you lose all sense of yourself, you can see only the blinding light which spreads everywhere, lighting up the layer of snow covering the glade, and igniting the flakes that are falling on us both like white powder.[28]

$\mathcal{H}$ildegard of Bingen bequeathed us the term *viriditas*, or "greening power." She talked and wrote of "the exquisite greening of trees and grasses" and how all of creation and humanity, in particular, is "showered with greening refreshment, the vitality to bear fruit." In a vision she had of the universe, Hildegard experienced what might be described as the metaphysical and unitive attributes of nature—a vision of nature as sacred Spirit of the cosmos, before it became profane. The Holy Spirit called upon her with these remarkable words:

I AM THAT SUPREME AND FIERY FORCE that sends forth all the sparks of life. Death hath no part in me, yet do I allot it, wherefore I am girt about with wisdom as with wings. I am that living and fiery essence of the divine substance that flows in the beauty of the fields. I shine in the water, I burn in the sun and the moon and the stars. Mine is that mysterious force of the invisible wind. I sustain the breath of all living. I breathe in the verdure and in the flowers, and when the waters flow like living things, it is I. I formed those columns that support the whole earth. . . . I am the force that lies hid in the winds, from me they take their source, and as a man may move because he breathes so doth a fire burn but by my blast. All these live because I am in them and am of their life. I am wisdom. Mine is the blast of the thundered word by which all things were made. I permeate all things that they may not die. I am life.[29]

*K*athleen Norris suggests how an improbable landscape of vast contradictions may function as a portal to "where it all comes together," in a meeting of heaven and earth within one's own soul.

A PERSON IS FORCED INWARD by the spareness of what is outward and visible in all this land and sky. The beauty of the Plains is like that of an icon; it does not give an inch to sentiment or romance. The flow of the land, with its odd twists and buttes, is like the flow of Gregorian chant that rises and falls beyond melody, beyond reason or human expectation, but perfectly.

Maybe seeing the Plains is like seeing an icon; what seems stern and almost empty is merely open, a door into some simple and holy state.[30]

The great Andalusian sage Ibn `Arabī (1165–1240) was born in Murcia in southern Spain into a family of pure Arab blood of the tribe of Tā'ī. His greatest "masterpiece" was his own life, writes Seyyed Hossein Nasr, "a most unusual life in which prayer, invocation, contemplation, and visits to various Sufi saints were combined with the theophanic vision of the spiritual world in which the invisible hierarchy was revealed to him."[31] In the Islamic world he was surnamed Muhyī al-Dīn, the Revivifier of Religion. His vision of the universe encompassed the principle of the universality of revelation, the idea that all prophets are an aspect of the Divine Presence—the Supreme Center—and that each, in fact, is "a logos" in him or her self. Ibn `Arabī believed in the transcendent unity of the inner core of all religions. Ultimately, he realized that divinely inspired paths all converge at the same peak, and that to have embraced a single faith completely is to have embraced them all; a recognition that has been immortalized in his famous and oft quoted poem:

My heart has become capable of every form: it is a pasture for
    gazelles and a convent for Christian monks,
And a temple for idols and the pilgrim's Ka'ba and the
    tables of the Torah, and the book of the Koran.
I follow the religion of Love: whatever way Love's camels take,
    that is my religion and my faith.[32]

Chaotic Roots

How marvellously man is made and formed if one penetrates into his true nature . . . and it is a great thing— consider for once, that there is nothing in heaven or in earth that is not also in man. . . . For He Himself says that He is in us, and that we are His temple.

PARACELSUS[33]

[A person] finds in his own being reflected in miniature, so to speak, the power, wisdom, and love of the Creator. If all the sages of the world were assembled, and their lives prolonged for an indefinite time, they could not effect any improvement in the construction of a single part of the body.

ABU HAMID MUHAMMAD AL-GHAZZALI (1058–1111),
PERSIAN VISIONARY AND SCHOLAR[34]

While teaching in the Himalayas, a Baul—an itinerant mystic and storyteller—recounts a pilgrimage he made as an old man to Badri Narayan, the land of Shiva, the Hindu god of procreation and destruction. He limns a journey into the multiple planes of being.

IT WAS A HARD CLIMB. I was almost dead with fatigue before reaching the summit; and I told my companions, "If I don't get there, leave me wherever I fall on Shiva's ground." But finally I got to the top and entered the temple. It was exactly like being swallowed by a huge whale, along with everything around me. Four or five others of our group entered at the same time and began to weep. I asked, "Why are you crying?" They couldn't answer. They had experienced something. As for me, I saw "That" with my eyes wide open; now I know it. Such was my pilgrimage toward the Mountain. I came back down again, but I am a different man.[35]

Is organized religion too inextricably bound to status quo to save our nation and the world? Maybe I must turn my faith to the inner spiritual church, the church within the church, as the true *ecclesia* and the hope of the world.

MARTIN LUTHER KING, JR. (1929–1968),
"LETTER FROM BIRMINGHAM CITY JAIL," 1963[36]

So it is on the spiritual path. Inner rejuvenation comes only when the outer vessel has been set in place. Then the very forms that originally seemed restrictive become liberating, for the practitioner has been freed from the fallen nature of reality. The rose of the tradition unfolds to reveal the presence of the Holy One within, and the flow of life released finds no better vehicle of expression than the very words of prayer one has been saying all along.

ELIEZER SHORE, WRITER AND TEACHER OF
JEWISH SPIRITUALITY IN JERUSALEM[37]

Eagle

[E]very great locality has its own pure daimon [attendant spirit], and is conveyed at last into perfected life. . . . Every great locality expresses itself perfectly, in its own flowers, its own birds and beasts, lastly its own men, with their perfected works. Mountains convey themselves in unutterable expressed perfection in the blue gentian flower and in the edelweiss flower, so soft, yet shaped like snow-crystals. The very strata of the earth come to a point of perfect, unutterable concentration in the inherent sapphires and emeralds. It is so with all worlds and all places of the world. We may take it as a law.

D. H. LAWRENCE (1885–1930), "THE SPIRIT OF PLACE"[38]

Notes

Epigraphs

1. See Gretel Ehrlich, "Landscape," Constance Sullivan, ed., *The Legacy of Light* (New York: Alfred A. Knopf, 1987), p. 20.
2. Anthony de Mello, *Awareness* (New York: Doubleday, 1990), p. 148.
3. Ansel Adams and Mary Street Alinder, *Ansel Adams: An Autobiography* (Boston: Little, Brown, 1985), p. 382.
4. Pierre Teilhard de Chardin, *The Future of Man* (New York: Harper & Row, 1969), p. 322.
5. See Karan Singh, *Essays on Hinduism* (Delhi: Ratna Sagar, 1990), p. 3.
6. Quoted in *The Temple of Understanding Newsletter,* Spring 1995, n.p.

Introduction

1. Ralph Waldo Emerson, "Self-Reliance," Carl Bode, ed., *The Portable Emerson* (New York: Viking Penguin, 1981), p. 141.
2. See Paul Devereux, *Earth Memory* (St. Paul, Minn.: Llewellyn Publications, 1992), pp. 148–49.
3. Very Rev. James Parks Morton, preface in *The Living Cathedral: St. John the Divine* (New York: Crossroad Publishing, 1993), p. 8.
4. Quoted in Aldous Huxley, *The Perennial Philosophy* (New York: New American Library, 1972), p. 69.
5. "Other joys," continues *The Catholic Encyclopedia,* "will be the sight of Christ's humanity, companionship with our Lord, the angels and the saints, and the understanding of creation."
6. Dante, *Paradise,* trans. Charles Eliot Norton (Boston: Houghton Mifflin, 1902), p. 208.
7. Walt Whitman, *Leaves of Grass,* ed. Harold W. Blodgett and Sculley Bradley (Chicago: University of Chicago Press, 1995), p. 471. See also Walt Whitman, "Poems of Joy," *The Blue Book: The 1860–61 Leaves of Grass* (New York: New York Public Library, 1968), p. 259.

8. Belden C. Lane, *Landscapes of the Sacred* (New York: Paulist Press, 1988), p. 15.

9. Mircea Eliade, *Patterns in Comparative Religion,* trans. Rosemary Sheed (New York: New American Library, 1974), p. 369.

10. Mircea Eliade, *The Sacred and the Profane: The Nature of Religion,* trans. William R. Trask (San Diego: Harcourt Brace Jovanovich, 1959), p. 13.

11. Amadou Hampâté Bâ, "Earth, Moon, and Sun," *Parabola,* vol. XIV, no. 3 (1989), pp. 49–50.

12. See T. C. McLuhan, *The Way of the Earth: Encounters with Nature in Ancient and Contemporary Thought* (New York: Simon & Schuster, 1994), p. 386.

13. Kevin J. Gilbert, *Because a White Man'll Never Do It* (Sydney: Angus & Robertson, 1973), p. 3.

14. Quoted in Stephen Hirst, *Havsuw'Baaja: People of the Blue Green Water* (Supai, Ariz.: The Havasupai Tribe, 1985), p. 204.

15. Quoted in Anita Parlow, *Cry, Sacred Ground: Big Mountain U.S.A.* (Washington, D.C.: The Christic Institute, 1985), p. 2.

16. Cosmas Okechukwu Obiego, *African Image of the Ultimate Reality: An Analysis of Igbo Ideas of Life and Death in Relation to Chunkwu-God* (Frankfurt am Main: Peter Lang, 1984), p. 144.

17. See McLuhan, *The Way of the Earth,* pp. 144–46; see also Daisetz Suzuki, *Japanese Spirituality,* trans. Norman Waddell (Tokyo: Japan Society for the Promotion of Science, 1972; New York: Greenwood Press, 1988).

18. Kostas Pasagianis, "Greek Travels," in Philip Sherrard, ed., *The Pursuit of Greece* (Athens: Denise Harvey & Co., 1987), pp. 168–69.

19. Ralph Waldo Emerson, "Worship," quoted in Richard G. Geldard, *The Esoteric Emerson* (Hudson, N.Y.: Lindisfarne Press, 1993), p. 177.

20. For an illuminating discussion on this topic, see Belden C. Lane, "Axioms for the Study of Sacred Space," *Landscapes of the Sacred,* pp. 11–33.

21. Quoted in *In Celebration of Trees,* a production of the Discovery Channel in association with Al Giddings Images Unlimited, Inc., 1991. Directed and photographed by Al Giddings. Produced by Terry Thompson and Sam Shore.

22. See William E. Geist, "Central Park: 5 Rms, No Fee, Great Breeze," in "About New York," *New York Times,* September 27, 1986.

23. Robert G. Lake, Jr. (Medicine Grizzly Bear), *Chilula: People from the Ancient Redwoods* (Washington, D.C.: University Press of America, 1982), p. 112. "Our old people used to walk in the deep forest to hear the secrets of life and talk to the Creator," continues Davis. "In the solitude and spirituality of the redwood forest their prayers would be answered."

24. See Michelle Gilbert, "The Sources of Power in Akuropon-Akuapem: Ambiguity in Classification," *Creativity of Power: Cosmology and Action in African Societies,* W.

Arens and Ivan Karp, eds. (Washington, D.C.: Smithsonian Institution Press, 1989), p. 59.

25. C. J. Jung, *Memories, Dreams, Reflections,* Aniela Jaffe, ed. (New York: Vintage Books, 1989), p. 198.

26. Hildegard of Bingen, *Illuminations of Hildegard of Bingen,* commentary by Matthew Fox (Santa Fe, N.M.: Bear & Company, 1985), p. 30.

27. James G. Cowan, *Letters from a Wild State: Rediscovering Our True Relationship to Nature* (New York: Bell Tower, 1991), p. 26.

28. For a lively discussion of what archaeologist Rachel Levy calls "the religion of the cave," see Rachel Levy, *The Gate of Horn: A Study of the Religious Conceptions of the Stone Age and Their Influence upon European Thought* (London: Faber & Faber, 1943). Levy theorizes that the deep prehistoric caverns were spiritual centers for initiation rites and other shamanistic rituals, and in this capacity, she proposes, they are organic expressions of the religious, artistic and social development—as well as achievement—of the ancient world before the Iron Age. Levy suggests the prehistoric caves represent a body of coherent ideas which have had a profound impact on succeeding civilizations.

29. Henry de Lumley, director of France's National Museum of Natural History, quoted in "Behold the Stone Age" in *Time,* February 13, 1995, p. 62.

30. Thomas Merton, *The Asian Journal,* Naomi Burton, Brother Patrick Hart, and James Laughlin, eds. (New York: New Directions, 1973), pp. 235–36. A description of Merton's pilgrimage to Mahabalipuram and Polonnaruwa (in Sri Lanka) is given in section 2, "Cathedrals Immemorial." At Polonnaruwa, the great buddha figures—motionless, silent, smiling, living shapes in full movement—left Merton stunned. "This is Asia in its purity," he wrote.

31. George William Russell (known as AE), *Song and Its Fountains* (New York: Macmillan, 1932), p. 7; also see AE quoted in Raynor C. Johnson, *The Light and the Gate* (London: Hodder and Stoughton, 1964), pp. 42–43.

32. Quoted in Stan Steiner, *The Vanishing White Man* (New York: Harper & Row, 1976), p.8.

33. Quoted in Frances Densmore, "Teton Sioux Music," Bureau of American Ethnology Bulletin no. 61 (1918), p. 214.

34. George William Russell, *The Candle of Vision* (New Hyde Park, N.Y.: University Books, 1965), p. 28.

35. Dōgen, *Shōbōgenzō: Zen Essays of Dōgen,* trans. Thomas Cleary (Honolulu: University of Hawaii Press, 1986).

36. Quoted in Alphonso Ortiz, *The Tewa World: Space, Time, Being and Becoming in a Pueblo Society* (Chicago: University of Chicago Press, 1969), p. 13.

37. Emanuel Swedenborg, *Heaven and Its Wonders and Hell* (New York: Swedenborg Foundation, 1980; first published in Latin, London, 1758), pp. 49–50.

38. See McLuhan, *The Way of the Earth*, p. 15.
39. Merton, *The Asian Journal*, p. 236.
40. Quoted in *Sanathana Sarathi*, February 1977, p. 271.
41. Teresa of Avila, *The Interior Castle*, trans. Kiernan Kavanaugh and Otilio Rodriguez (New York: Paulist Press, 1979), p. 21.
42. Richard R. Niebuhr, "Pilgrims and Pioneers," *Parabola*, vol. IX, no. 3 (1984), p. 7.
43. Richard Leviton, "Designing Your Pilgrimage," *Quest*, vol. 7, no. 4 (1994), pp. 25–29.

   The Venerable Tara Tulku, a Tibetan Buddhist monk, states that the expression for "pilgrimage" in Tibetan is "to turn around the place," to circumambulate a place. He says that "the Dharma itself is circling around the globe. The whole globe is becoming a Wheel of Dharma." (See interview with Tara Tulku in *Parabola*, vol. IX, no. 3, 1984.)

44. Dorothy Day, *On Pilgrimage* (New York: Catholic Worker Books, 1948), pp. 59, 126, 138.
45. Hermann Hesse, *The Journey to the East* (New York: Farrar, Straus and Giroux, 1968), pp. 12–13.
46. *Desert Stories*, a half-hour documentary film about the Pintupi people of central Australia, 1984. The film focuses on some engaging Pintupi elders and their stories around the Papunya Aboriginal Settlement near Alice Springs in central Australia. Directed and edited by Lindsay Frazer; written and narrated by Billy Marshall-Stoneking; produced by Nick Frazer. Network 0/28. Special Broadcasting Service, 1984.
47. All statements by photographer Eliot Bowen from are conversations, interviews, and correspondence with the author.

Arboreal Cathedrals

1. Quoted in Soiku Shigematsu, comp. and trans., *A Zen Forest* (New York and Tokyo: Weatherhill, 1981), p. 120.
2. See Charles Fenyvesi, *Trees* (New York: St. Martin's Press, 1992), prefatory quote.
3. James G. Cowan, *Letters from a Wild State:* Rediscovering Our True Relationship to Naure (New York: Bell Tower, 1991), pp. 88–89, 96.
4. Satish Kumar, *No Destination* (Bideford, Devon: Resurgence, 1992), p. 183.
5. Matsuo Bashō in Makoto Ueda, *Matsuo Bashō* (New York: Twayne Publishers, 1970), p. 137.
6. Quoted in Aldous Huxley, *The Perennial Philosophy* (New York: New American Library, 1972), p. 69.
7. Quoted in Geoffrey Keynes, ed., *The Letters of William Blake* (Cambridge: Harvard University Press, 1968), p. 31.

8. William Blake in Keynes, *Letters of William Blake,* p. 30.

9. George Seferis, *Poems,* trans. Rex Warner (Boston: Nonpareil Books, 1978), p. 49.

10. See Naveen Patnaik, *The Garden of Life: An Introduction to the Healing Plants of India* (New York: Doubleday, 1993), p. 23.

11. Ibid., p. 16.

12. Ibid.

13. Ibid., p. 23.

14. Quoted in Evelyn Underhill, *Mysticism* (New York: New American Library, 1974), pp. 190–91.

15. Laurens van der Post, in conversation with Jean-Marc Pottiez, *A Walk with a White Bushman* (London: Chatto & Windus, 1986), p. 3.

16. Quoted in Frederic I. Carpenter, *Laurens van der Post* (New York: Twayne Publishers, 1969), p. 15.

17. Laurens van der Post, *A Far-Off Place* (New York: William Morrow, 1974), pp. 79–80.

18. See Steven C. Rockefeller and John C. Elder, eds., *Spirit and Nature* (Boston: Beacon Press, 1992), p. 174.

19. Allen Meredith in Anand Chetan and Diane Brueton, *The Sacred Yew* (Harmondsworth: Penguin, 1994), p. 12.

20. Rabindranath Tagore in Amiya Chakravarty, ed., *A Tagore Reader* (New York: The Macmillan Company, 1961), p. 279.

21. Ibid., p. 87.

22. Natalie Curtis, ed., *The Indians' Book* (New York: Harper and Brothers, 1923; New York: Dover Publications, 1968), p. 11.

23. For a detailed, authoritative, and fascinating account of the life of Hildegard of Bingen see Mother Columba Hart and Jane Bishop, *Hildegard of Bingen* (New York: Paulist Press, 1990).

24. Hildegard of Bingen, in ibid., p. 124.

25. *The Wisdom of the Desert Fathers,* trans. Sister Benedicta Ward (Oxford: SLG Press, 1975), p. 43.

26. Chief John Snow, *These Mountains Are Our Sacred Places* (Toronto: Samuel Stevens, 1977), pp. 146–47.

27. Matsuo Bashō, *The Narrow Road to the Deep North,* trans. Nobuyuki Yuasa (Harmondsworth: Penguin Books, 1966), p. 26.

28. George Clutesi, *Potlatch* (Sidney, British Columbia: Gray's Publishing, 1969), p.89.

29. Opal Whiteley, "The Joy-Song of Nature," in Benjamin Hoff, ed., *The Singing Creek Where the Willows Grow: The Rediscovered Diary of Opal Whitely* (New York: Ticknor & Fields, 1986; first published in 1920 as *The Story of Opal: The Journal of an Understanding Heart*), pp. 59–60. See also Lorraine Anderson, ed., *Sisters of the Earth: Women's Prose and Poetry About Nature* (New York: Vintage, 1991).

30. Kofi Awoonor, *Comes the Voyager at Last: A Tale of Return to Africa* (Trenton, N.J.: Africa World Press, 1992), p. 43.
31. Patnaik, *Garden of Life*, p. 153.
32. Henry David Thoreau, "Walking," *The Natural History Essays* (Salt Lake City: Peregrine Smith, 1980), p. 116.
33. AE, *The Candle of Vision* (New Hyde Park, N.Y.: University Books 1986), p. 170.
34. George William Russell's meditations on the "holy substance they call common clay," the Mighty Mother Earth, appear throughout his two volumes, *The Candle of Vision* and *Song and Its Fountains*, from which these thoughts are culled. See *Song and Its Fountains* (New York: Macmillan, 1932), p. 7; *Candle of Vision*, pp. 32–33.
35. George Nakashima, *The Soul of a Tree: A Woodworker's Reflections* (New York: Kodansha International, 1981), pp. xxi, 81, 84.
36. Quoted in Richard Wilhelm, trans., *The Secret of the Golden Flower: A Chinese Book of Life* (New York: Harcourt Brace Jovanovich; a Harvest/HBJ book, 1962), p. 128.
37. Stephanie Kaza, *The Attentive Heart: Conversations with Trees* (New York: Fawcett Columbine, 1993), p. 157.
38. Ibid., p. 152.
39. Ibid., pp. 154–55.
40. Paracelsus in Jolande Jacobi, ed., *Paracelsus: Selected Writings*, Bollingen Series XXVIII (New York: Pantheon, 1951), p. 183.
41. See Karan Singh, *Essays on Hinduism* (Delhi: Ratna Sagar, 1990), pp. 1–3.
42. Quoted in Patnaik, *Garden of Life*, p. 7.
43. Quoted in Claire Holt, *Art in Indonesia: Continuities and Change* (Ithaca, N.Y.: Cornell University Press, 1967), p. 76.
44. "Readers Write About 'Trees,'" *The Sun*, August 1991, pp. 24–25.
45. Patnaik, *Garden of Life*, p. 24.
46. Ibid.
47. Rainer Maria Rilke, translated by Albert Ernest Flemming, *Selected Poems* (New York: Routledge, 1990), p. 28.
48. See E. A. Wallis Budge, *An Egyptian Reading Book* (London: Kegan Paul, Trench, Trubner, 1896; New York: AMS Press, 1976), p. xxi.
49. Diane Wolkstein, *The Magic Orange Tree* (New York: Schocken Books, 1980), p. 14.
50. Rainer Maria Rilke, *Selected Works, Prose*, vol. 1, trans. G. Craig Houston (London: Hogarth Press, 1954), pp. 34–36.
51. Forrest Carter, *The Education of Little Tree* (New York: Delacorte, 1976), pp. 61–62. For details concerning the factual and/or fictional character of the book, see McLuhan, *The Way of the Earth* (pp. 389, 511) and Lawrence Clayton, "Forrest Carter/Asa Carter and Politics," *Western American Literature*, May 1986, pp. 19–26.
52. Tagore in Chakravarty, *Tagore Reader*, p. 328.

53. Quoted in Chiang Yee, *The Chinese Eye* (Bloomington: Indiana University Press, 1964), p. 96.
54. Patnaik, *Garden of Life*, p. 37.
55. Ibid.
56. Quoted in Huxley, *Perennial Philosophy*, p. 69.
57. Robert Walshe, *Wales' Work* (New York: Ticknor & Fields, 1986), p. 257.
58. Quoted in Chetan and Brueton, *Sacred Yew*, p. 19.
59. Sir George Trevelyan, Foreword, in ibid., pp. xi–xii.
60. Quoted in Patnaik, *Garden of Life*, p. 19.
61. Quoted in Howard Mumford Jones, *O Strange New World: American Culture: The Formative Years* (New York: Viking, 1965), pp. 14–15.

Cathedrals Immemorial

1. Gretel Erhlich, "Landscape," Constance Sullivan, ed., *The Legacy of Light* (New York: Alfred A. Knopf, 1987), p. 17.
2. Al-Ghazzali in Syed Nawab Ali, *Some Moral and Religious Teachings of Al-Ghazzali* (Lahore: Sh. Muhammad Ashraf, 1920), p. 120.
3. Marco Pallis, *The Way and the Mountain* (London: Peter Owen, 1961), pp. 25–26.
4. Laurens van der Post in conversation with Jean-Marc Pottiez, *A Walk with a White Bushman* (London: Chatto & Windus, 1986), p. 317.
5. Jack McPhee in Sally Morgan, *Wanamurraganya: The Story of Jack McPhee* (Fremantle, Australia: Fremantle Arts Centre Press, 1989), pp. 58–59.
6. C. G. Jung, *Memories, Dreams, Reflections* (New York: Vintage Books, 1989), pp. 255–56.
7. An interview with Tara Tulku, Rinpoche, "A New Dwelling," in *Parabola*, vol. IX, no. 3 (1984), pp. 30–39.
8. See Columba Stewart, trans., *The World of the Desert Fathers* (Oxford: SLG Press, 1986), pp. 40–41.
9. Thomas Miller, *Desert Skin* (Salt Lake City: University of Utah Press, 1994), pp. 93–95.
10. See Barbara Novak, *The Ape & the Whale* (Moose, Wyo.: Homestead Publishing, 1995), p. 75.
11. Ibid., p. 80.
12. Ibid., pp. 21–22.
13. Clive James, ed., *Vedanta: An Anthology of Hindu Scriptures, Commentary, and Poetry* (New York: Bantam, 1974), p. 5.
14. Thomas Merton, *The Asian Journal*, Naomi Burton, Brother Patrick Hart, and James Laughlin, eds. (New York: New Directions, 1973), p. 236.

15. Ibid., p. 230.
16. Ibid., pp. 233–36.
17. Ibid., p. xxiii.
18. Ibid., pp. 197–98, 235–36.
19. Anand Chetan and Diane Brueton, *The Sacred Yew* (Harmondsworth: Penguin, 1994), p. 8.
20. Seyyed Hossein Nasr, *Islamic Art and Spirituality* (Albany: State University of New York Press, 1987), p. 196.
21. Ibid., p. 202.
22. Ibid., pp. 39, 183.
23. Rina Swentzell, *An Understated Sacredness*. From the series *Colores,* a KNME TV 5 production, Albuquerque, New Mexico, 1992. The shrines, explains Swentzell, act as contact points between the various realms of existence in Pueblo culture. "The shrines, boundary markers and centers [that saturate Pueblo community life]," she says, "then serve as constant reminders of the religious, symbolic nature of life."
24. See Unni Wikan, *Managing Turbulent Hearts: A Balinese Formula for Living* (Chicago: University of Chicago Press, 1990), p. 166.
25. John Wesley Powell, introduction by Wallace Stegner, *The Exploration of the Colorado River and Its Canyons* (first published in the United States as *Canyons of the Colorado* in 1875; New York: Penquin Books, 1987), p. 397. Intoxicated by the otherworldly beauty of the canyon, Powell rhapsodizes: "The Grand Canyon is a land of song. Mountains of music swell in the rivers, hills of music billow in the creeks, and meadows of music murmur in the rills that ripple over the rocks. Altogether it is a symphony of multitudinous melodies. All this is the music of waters. The adamant foundations of the earth have been wrought into a sublime harp, upon which the clouds of the heavens play with mighty tempests or with gentle showers" (pp. 394, 397).
26. From Kofi Awoonor's unpublished manuscript, *A Memoir*. With the permission of the author.
27. See *AICH Community Bulletin,* Spring 1995, p. 13.
28. Matsuo Bashō in Nobuyuki Yuasa, trans., *The Narrow Road to the Deep North* (Harmondsworth: Penguin, 1966), p. 122.
29. John Blofeld, *The Wheel of Life: The Autobiography of a Western Buddhist* (Boston: Shambhala, 1988), p. 117.
30. Ibid., pp. 116–17.
31. Stephanie Kaza, *The Attentive Heart: Conversations with Trees* (New York: Fawcett Columbine, 1993), p. 128.
32. James G. Cowan, *Letters from a Wild State: Rediscovering Our True Relationship to Nature* (New York: Bell Tower, 1991), pp. 117–18.
33. Yi-Fu Tuan, *Topophilia: A Study of Environmental Perception, Attitudes, and Values* (Englewood Cliffs, N.J.: Prentice-Hall, 1974).

34. Lama Anagarika Govinda, *The Way of the White Clouds* (London: Rider & Co., 1992), pp. 45–46.

35. Lex Hixon, *The Heart of the Koran* (Wheaton, Ill.: The Theosophical Publishing House, 1988), pp. 18–20.

36. See James Bishop, *Epitaph for a Desert Anarchist: The Life and Legacy of Edward Abbey* (New York: Atheneum, 1994), prefatory quote.

Open-Air Cathedrals

1. Gretel Erhlich, *The Solace of Open Spaces* (New York: Viking, 1985), p. 14.

2. See T. C. McLuhan, *The Way of the Earth* (New York: Simon & Schuster, 1994), p. 409.

3. Edward Abbey, *Desert Solitaire* (Tucson: University of Arizona Press, 1988), pp. 163–64.

4. Belden C. Lane, *Landscapes of the Sacred* (New York: Paulist Press, 1988), pp. 13–14.

5. Gretel Ehrlich, "Landscape," in Constance Sullivan, ed., *The Legacy of Light* (New York: Alfred A. Knopf, 1987), pp. 20, 21.

6. Chiang Yee, *The Chinese Eye* (Bloomington: Indiana University Press, 1964), pp. 9–10, 13.

7. Quoted in Lane, *Landscapes of the Sacred*, p. vii.

8. Kazuaki Tanahashi, *Brush Mind* (Berkeley, Calif.: Parallax Press, 1990), p. 131.

9. Muso Soseki, "Temple of Eternal Light," *Sun at Midnight: Poems and Sermons by Muso Soseki*, trans. W. S. Merwin and Soiku Shigematsu (San Francisco: North Point Press, 1989), p. 122.

10. Abbey, *Desert Solitaire*, pp. 171–72.

11. See Chiang Yee, *The Chinese Eye*, p. 92.

12. Oren Lyons also works for the United Nations Global Forum and uses an Iroquois passport to travel throughout the world. He is quoted here from an interview in the TBS series *The Native Americans*, Part One, October 1994.

13. AE, "Ireland Behind the Veil," Raghavan Iyer and Nandini Iyer, eds., *The Descent of the Gods* (Gerrards Cross, Buckinghamshire: Colin Smythe, 1988), pp. 637–38.

14. Li Po, "On the Mountain: Question and Answer," Cyril Birch, ed., *Anthology of Chinese Literature* (New York: Grove, 1965), p. 242.

15. Ch'an master Hui Hai, *The Zen Teaching of Hui Hai*, trans. John Blofeld (London: Rider & Company, 1962), p. 111.

16. Sharon Butala, *The Perfection of the Morning: An Apprenticeship in Nature* (Toronto: HarperCollins, 1994), pp. 216–17.

17. See W. A. Braarem, collected by, *Luo Zaho: Indonesian Poetry* (Port Moresby: Papua Pocket Poets, 1967), p. 7.

18. C. Hooykaas, *Cosmogony and Creation in Balinese Tradition* (The Hague: Martinus Nijhoff, 1974), p. 149.

19. Marco Pallis, *The Way and the Mountain* (London: Peter Owen, 1961), p. 112.

20. Ibid., pp. 112–13.

21. Quoted in Chiang Yee, *The Chinese Eye*, p. 135.

22. George William Russell, "Ireland Behind the Veil," *Universal Brotherhood*, June 1897; reprinted in Katherine Tingley, ed., *The Theosophical Path* (Point Loma, Calif.), vol. XXII, no. 3 (March 1922); also reprinted in Iyer and Iyer, *Descent of the Gods*, pp. 639–40.

23. Quoted in Evelyn Underhill, *Mysticism* (New York: New American Library, 1974), p. 208.

24. Tessa Bielecki, "Bridal Mysticism," Susan Walker, ed., *Speaking of Silence* (New York: Paulist Press, 1987), pp. 40, 42.

25. Julian Lang, ed. and trans., *Ararapikva: Creation Stories of the People* (Berkeley, Calif.: Heyday Books, 1994), pp. 9, 22–25.

26. Kathleen Norris, *Dakota: A Spiritual Geography* (Boston: Houghton Mifflin Company, 1993), pp. 15, 17–19.

27. John Blofeld, *The Wheel of Life: The Autobiography of a Western Buddhist* (Boston: Shambhala Publications, 1988), p. 118.

28. Ibid., p. 151.

29. Ibid., p. 15.

30. Amy Barratt, "The Mountain," *The Antigonish Review*, no. 99, Autumn 1994, p. 136.

31. Lama Anagarika Govinda, *The Way of the White Clouds* (London: Rider & Co., 1992), p. 62.

32. Thomas Berry, "The Meadow Across the Creek," unpublished manuscript. With permission from the author.

33. Ralph Waldo Emerson, *English Traits* (Boston: Phillips, Sampson, and Company, 1857), p. 55.

34. Quoted in Jolande Jacobi, ed., *Paracelsus: Selected Writings,* Bollingen Series XXVIII (New York: Pantheon, 1951), p. 50.

The Cathedrals Within

1. Thomas Merton, *The Asian Journal,* Naomi Burton, Brother Patrick Hart, and James Laughlin, eds. (New York: New Directions, 1973), p. xxix.

2. Quoted in Richard Maurice Bucke, *Cosmic Consciousness* (Secaucus, N.J.: Citadel Press, 1982), p. 169.

3. See Richard Wilhelm, trans., *The Secret of the Golden Flower: A Chinese Book of Life* (New York: Harcourt Brace Jovanovich; a Harvest/HBJ book, 1962), p. 106.

"These visions which I saw," wrote Hildegard, "I beheld neither in sleep, nor in dream, nor in madness, nor with my carnal eyes, nor with the ears of the flesh, nor in hidden places; but wakeful, alert, with the eyes of the spirit and with the inward ears I perceived them in open view and according to the will of God. And how this was compassed is hard indeed for human flesh to search out." (See Charles Singer, "The Scientific Views and Visions of Saint Hildegard," in *Studies in the History and Method of Science* [London: William Dawson & Sons, 1955], p. 53.)

4. Rabindranath Tagore, in Amiya Chakravarty, ed., *A Tagore Reader* (New York: The Macmillan Company, 1961), p. 225.

5. Ibid., pp. 84, 86.

6. Nikos Kazantzakis, *Saint Francis* (New York: Simon & Schuster, 1962), pp. 176–77.

7. See Joseph Campbell, ed., *The Portable Jung* (New York: Penguin, 1976), p. 524. See also *Tertullian, Apologetical Works,* Library of the Fathers of the Church (New York: Fathers of the Church, 1950), p. 140.

8. See Barbara Novak, *The Ape & the Whale* (Moose, Wyo.: Homestead Publishing, 1995), pp. 91–92.

9. Blanche Howard, "A Good Day on a Minor Galaxy," *The Antigonish Review*, no. 99, Autumn 1994, pp. 13–14.

10. Quoted in Jane Hirshfield, ed., *Women in Praise of the Sacred* (New York: Harper-Collins, 1994), p. 109.

11. Anthony de Mello, *The Song of the Bird* (New York: Doubleday, 1982), pp. 22–23.

12. Stephanie Kaza, *The Attentive Heart: Conversations with Trees* (New York: Fawcett Columbine, 1993), pp. 149–50.

13. Quoted in *The John Main Newsletter*, Dom Laurence Freeman's letter of March 21, 1995, p. 2.

14. See A. J. Arberry, *Sufism: An Account of the Mystics of Islam* (London: Unwin Paperbacks, 1979), pp. 54–55.

15. Saul Bellow, "Reflections (The Middle East-I)," *The New Yorker*, July 12, 1976, pp. 43–44. See also Saul Bellow, *To Jerusalem and Back: A Personal Account* (New York: Viking Penguin, 1976), p. 10.

16. Thomas Buckley, "Living in the Distance," *Parabola*, vol. IX, no. 3 (1984), p. 73.

17. *Songs of Kabir*, trans. Rabindranath Tagore (1917; reprint, New Delhi: Cosmo, 1985), p. 45.

18. Claude Lévi-Strauss, *Tristes Tropiques* (New York: Atheneum, 1974), p. 142.

19. Quoted in Aldous Huxley, *The Perennial Philosophy* (New York: New American Library, 1972), pp. 74–75.

20. Ibid., p. 170.

21. Howard Murphet, *Where the Road Ends* (Madras: Macmillan, 1993), pp. 182–83.

22. e. e. cummings, in Rolphe Humphries, ed., *New Poems by American Poets #2* (New

York: Ballantine, 1957), p. 39. See also *Complete Poems: 1905–1962 by E. E. Cummings,* ed. George J. Firmage (London: Marchim Press, 1973), p. 749.

23. See Rabindranath Tagore, *The Religion of Man* (Boston: Beacon Press, 1961), p. 190.

24. Naveen Patnaik, *The Garden of Life: An Introduction to the Healing Plants of India* (New York: Doubleday, 1993), p. 71.

25. See George A. Maloney S.J., *Prayer of the Heart* (Notre Dame, Ind.: Ave Maria Press, 1981), p. 168. Nyssa was a name that embraced several ancient cities devoted to the worship of Dionysus. Cappadocia, the town in which Gregory was reared by an aristocratic Christian family, was the best-known settlement located in what is now east-central Asiatic Turkey.

26. Quoted in Huxley, *Perennial Philosophy,* p. 174.

27. Thomas Merton, *The Sign of Jonas* (New York: Harcourt Brace Jovanovich; a Harvest/HBJ book, 1979), p. 360. The author of more than forty books and pamphlets and several collections of poetry, Thomas Merton is perhaps best known for his inspirational and witty biographical account of seeking monkhood amidst the pratfalls of day-to-day life so humanly described in his *The Seven Storey Mountain.*

28. Valentine Zander, *St. Seraphim Sarov* (Crestwood, N.Y.: St. Vladimir's Seminary Press, 1975), p. 91.

29. Quoted in Charles Singer, "The Scientific Views and Visions of Saint Hildegard," in *Studies in the History and Method of Science* (Oxford: Oxford University Press, vol. 1, 1917), p. 33. As she was nearing the end of her life, Hildegard wrote that the living light never really deserted her, as she came to recognize that she and it were in accord:

And now that I am over seventy years old my spirit according to the will of God soars upward in vision to the highest heaven and to the farthest stretch of the air and spreads itself among different peoples to regions exceeding far from me here, and thence I can behold the changing clouds and the mutations of all created things; for all these I see not with the outward eye or ear, nor do I create them from the cogitations of my heart . . . but within my spirit, my eyes being open, so that I have never suffered any terror when they left me." (Singer, p. 55).

30. Kathleen Norris, *Dakota: A Spiritual Geography* (Boston: Houghton Mifflin Company, 1993), p. 157.

31. Seyyed Hossein Nasr, *Three Muslim Sages* (Cambridge, Mass.: Harvard University Press, 1964), p. 92.

32. Quoted in ibid., p. 118.

33. Jolande Jacobi, ed., *Paracelsus: Selected Writings,* Bollingen Series XXVIII (New York: Pantheon, 1951), p. 119.

34. Abu Hamid Muhammad al-Ghazzali, trans. Claud Field, rev. and annotated by Elton L. Daniel, *The Alchemy of Happiness* (Armonk, N.Y.: M.E. Sharpe, 1991), p. 15.

35. Quoted in Lizelle Reymond, "Intimate Journeys," *Parabola*, vol. IX, no. 3, (August 1984), p. 41. See also *To Live Within*, Reymond's account of her five-year stay in a Himalayan hermitage. *Hima* and *laya* are Sanskrit words meaning "abode of snow."
36. Martin Luther King, Jr., "Letter from Birmingham City Jail," in Hillman M. Bishop and Samuel Hendel, eds., *Basic Issues of American Democracy: A Book of Readings* (New York: Appleton-Century-Crofts, 1965), pp. 288–96.
37. Eliezer Shore, "The Heart of Ritual," *Parabola*, vol. XIX, no. 4, (1994), p. 20.
38. D. H. Lawrence, *Studies in Classic American Literature* (New York: The Viking Press, 1964), p. 30.

PICTURE LEGEND

Cover photo: *An Assemblage of Elders*. Arches National Park, Red Rock Country of south-eastern Utah. June 1995.

page 24
Reclining Woman. Millicoma River Valley, east of Coos Bay, Oregon. May 1993.

page 27
Call of the Stones. Also known as *Balanced Rock(s)*; Arches National Park, Utah. July 1993. "Arches" includes approximately 114 square miles of semi-desert country, a fantastic and outlandish terrain where improbability dominates. The sculpted landscape of dramatic erosional landforms features innumerable natural arches, hypnotic spires and fin-like shapes, pinnacles, towering buttes and megaliths, ancient Indian ruins, petrified sand dunes, and a multitude of animal and plant life. The *balanced rock* monolith in the foreground of the photograph rises to a total elevation of 128 feet. The rock boulder atop the Entrada sandstone base is 55 feet in height and weighs almost 3,577 tons, or in the words of Arches writer and historian John Hoffman, "the equivalent of 1,600 automobiles." The boulder is fastened naturally to its pedestal and, with time, will topple. Arches' unique life-like landforms range in age from 300 million to 100 million years. Many bear resemblances to mythical creatures, animals and humans.

page 31
Running Tree. Japanese Garden, Golden Gate Park, San Francisco. May 1993.

page 37
Ent. Hoh Rain Forest, Olympic Peninsula, Washington. March 1995. In J. R. R. Tolkien's *The Lord of the Rings*, the *Ents* are treelike creatures of the forest with "rootlike toes" and long-term memory; "trees and *Ents* . . . walk down the ages together." They resemble a large variety of trees, including the beech, linden, fir, and birch. *Ents* are the guardians of trees as well as of those who think and feel as they do.

page 41
Walking Stone Guardians. "Avenue of Stones," Avebury, England. January 1989.

page 46
Tree Spirit. Seward Park, Seattle. 1992.

page 50

Old Man of the Hoh. Hoh Rain Forest, Olympic Peninsula, Washington. January 1990. The word "Hoh" derives from an Indian word that means "fast white water." The temperate-zone Hoh Rain Forest is part of Olympic National Park of the Pacific Northwest. Glaciers, seashore, herds of elk, and forests are a part of this unique woodland that was incorporated into a National Park on June 29, 1938 by President Franklin D. Roosevelt.

page 54

Tree Awakening. Mayfair Newell Park, Seattle. April 1992.

page 60

Green Man. Hoh Rain Forest. Olympic Peninsula, Washington. September 1992. An archetypal image from pre-history, the *Green Man* signifies boundless life. He is a symbol of a oneness re-membered. "His words are leaves," says poet and author William Anderson. "He knows and utters the secret laws of Nature." The *Green Man* exhibits a synergy of human and arborescent characteristics. Thick curtains of clubmoss enshroud and favor the giant bigleaf maples of the Hoh creating their own mysterious sculptures and dramatic forms of which this is one. Finer draperies of epiphytes (mosses, clubmosses, and lichens) produce delicate weavings and configurations of enchantment that hang from the limbs of the towering Sitka spruce, western red cedar, douglas fir, and western hemlock—the "Big Four" of the Hoh Rain Forest.

page 63

Torso. Washington Square Park, New York City. August 1995.

page 68

Embracing Roots. Chan Chich, Belize, Central America. 1990. Situated in the northwest corner of Belize—a country of 8,800 square miles and a population of less than 200,000—Chan Chich is a pilgrim's paradisiacal refuge set within a tropical forest and virgin wilderness area that extends over 250,000 acres and includes an ancient Mayan city with its central plaza, temples and burial mounds dating ca. A.D. 250–800. More than 700 species of trees flourish in the forest together with some 4,000 plant species. Chan Chich is the name of a little river that winds its way through the forest. It also means "little bird" in an old Mayan song.

page 71

Redwood Sage. Northern California. May 1993.

page 78

Pachyderm. Standing Stone with Burial Mound in Distance, "Avenue of Stones;" Avebury, England. January 1989. The grand earthwork and stone circles of Avebury located on the Marlborough chalk downs of Wiltshire in southern England have been called "the open-air temples of prehistoric Britain." All the stones are sarsen, a hard type of sandstone. It is thought that a total of more than 400 stones stood at one time both within the earthwork (made up of a massive ditch and bank) and outside in the two avenues—each with a double row of standing stones—which may have been used in antiquity as processional pathways. The largest surviving stone weighs almost 60 tons; the average being 15 tons. The height of the megaliths varies tremendously, ranging from 4 to 22 feet. The stone circles of the Avebury complex were most probably constructed ca. 2400 B.C. They span an area of approximately 28½ acres. It has been suggested that they were important religious and ceremonial sites. Astronomical significance has also been attached to the circles. The full purpose and function of Avebury, however, remains a mystery.

page 84

Ecstatic Tree. University of Washington Arboretum, Japanese Garden, Seattle. 1992.

page 87

"Adam and Eve." Two surviving stones of "The Cove," Avebury Circle, Avebury, England. January 1989. At the center of the North Circle, and thought to be its central shrine, are two impressive megaliths, known as the Longstones, or "Adam and Eve." Their purpose remains an enigma. In 1911, "Adam" was re-erected and weighed in at more than 30 tons. The diameter of the northern inner circle measured about 320 feet and contained approximately 27 stones of which four are visible today. The original configuration of "The Cove" consisted of three great stones that formed three sides of a square. The missing stone was said to have been a "full seven yards long." "Adam" is 16 feet high; the "Eve" stone is 10 feet in height.

page 92

Tree Hands. Chan Chich, Belize, Central America. 1990.

page 97

Feline Spirit. Commonwealth Avenue, Boston. Summer 1990.

page 104

Baucis and Philemon. Chan Chich, Belize, Central America. 1990.
According to Greek legend (in Rex Warner's *The Stories of the Greeks*), Philemon and his wife, Baucis, who lived in a humble house in Phrygia, gave their unstinting hospitality to the gods Jupiter and Mercury when all the other townspeople refused to offer them food and a place to rest. In return, the gods granted them their fondest wish: to die at the same moment and thus be spared the sorrow of living without the other. One day when they were very old, each noticed that bark was beginning to cover their bodies and leaves were growing from them as though they were becoming trees. Before the bark closed over their faces, they cried out happily: "Goodbye, dear wife," and "Goodbye, dear husband." Peasants in Phrygia to this day show travelers the two trees they insist are Baucis and Philemon—still growing together, side by side, their branches and trunks intertwined.

page 108

The Hooting Cairn. Kenidzhek, Penwith Peninsula, Cornwall, England. January 1989. Described as a strange brooding place, the "Hooting Cairn" received its name from its haunting legends and "probably from the significant prophetic noises which consecrated rocks were supposed by the ancients sometimes to emit," says Dr. William Borlase in *Antiquities of Cornwall* (1754). The dramatic Kenidzhek Cairn towers above the landscape and is thought to have had astronomical functions.

page 111
Pantheon. Rock monolith in Vedauwoo Recreation Area, Medicine Bow Mountains, southeast Wyoming.

page 115
Glastonbury Tor, Sacred Spiral Hill. Glastonbury, Somerset, England. January 1989. It is an inspiration when one first catches sight of the classic sacred hill, a great breast of the earth, that rises to a height of 522 feet and dominates the surrounding landscape. The renowned holy Tor (the word "Tor" is of Celtic origin meaning rocky peak or lofty conical hill) is the locus of numerous wells, the most famous being the ancient Chalice Well, a powerful source for healing. Mysterious labyrinthine ridges spiral their way around the hill. It has been suggested that they were used as initiation paths; perhaps a spirit concourse. The ruins of a 14th century chapel dedicated to St. Michael rest on top of the Tor.

page 118
Buddha Nature. Central Pillar (with shell and feather offerings at the base of the stone megalith), Boscawen-un Circle, Penwith Peninsula, Cornwall, England. January 1989. The arresting central megalith of granite is wreathed by a necklace of 19 stones also of granite—with the exception of one which is a shining block of white quartz. The capacity of crystals to interact with consciousness is a widely held belief in a multitude of traditions across the planet. Quartz and rock crystal, for example, have been used in traditional cultures as catalysts for healing and clairvoyance since antiquity. Granite possesses innate radioactivity which is known to induce altered states and visible light.

page 125
Lizards in Love. On the beach at Marenco Biological Reserve, southwest Pacific Coast, Costa Rica. February 1995.

page 132
Cornish Lingam. Standing Stone at Trelew Farm, between Drift and St. Buryan, Cornwall, England. January 1989. One of the principal Hindu deities in India is Shiva, destroyer and creator of worlds, and symbolically represented by a phallic pillar called a lingam. The phallus symbolized power, fertility, continuity; in other words, existence. Burial megaliths, phallic in form, are found in cultures across the world and were intended to protect the life of the deceased spirit. "The soul 'dwelt' in the stone," writes Mircea Eliade, "and that is why, in so many cultures, stones thought to be inhabited by 'ancestors' are instruments for fertilizing fields and women." The old stones appear to thrive in the fields around St. Buryan. The tall pillar at Trelew was excavated in 1871 by the local scholar and clergyman, Dr. William Borlase, who found fragments of human bones close to its northern face.

The scientist Sir Norman Lockyer and engineer Alexander Thom visited, surveyed and wrote about the Cornish monuments (at the turn of the century and in the 1960s respectively) identifying them as alignment sites and instruments for astronomical observation. Lockyer was the first to re-ascribe such attributes to the monuments. The professional and committed work of both Lockyer and Thom created waves of enthusiasm for megalithic sites, an experience that author John Michel infectiously calls "megalithomania."

page 137

Elves in the Trees. Hoh Rain Forest, Olympic Peninsula, Washington. March 1995. More than 130 species of epiphytes thrive on Hoh trees adorning the forest's branches with six to ten inches of luxuriant greenscape while spinning their intriguing shapes and archways. The epiphytes (Greek for "on plants") obtain their own nourishment from rainwater and the air and provide their host tree with valuable nutrients.

page 139

Wishing Stone. Avebury Circle, Avebury, England. January 1989. This gigantic sarsen measures approximately 14 feet wide and 13 feet high. It is the only Avebury megalith possessing "a top aperture," reports author Michael Dames in *The Avebury Circle*. "It is a portal stone," writes Dames, "and physical portals are often psychological thresholds." Locally, the stone is known as the "Devil's Chair" because it incorporates a small ledge in the lower central part of the megalith, large enough for a sitter. Until the 1930s, says Dames, the stone continued to exert a seasonal influence over the future of adolescent girls and hence was called the "Wishing Stone." It is still considered by some an instrument of divination.

page 142

Languorous Nude. Chan Chich, Belize, Central America. 1990.

page 144

Chun Quoit. Land's End, Cornwall, England. January 1989. Located on a hilltop of open moorland near the toppled stones of the ancient enclosure Chun Castle, this granite monument is often referred to as a megalithic mushroom. Its near circular twelve-foot-in-diameter capstone covers a complete chamber. The box-like triadic form constructed from uprights and slabs is called a dolmen but in Cornish country is known as a "Quoit." Chun Quoit is an impressive Iron Age structure that appears to be crafted from "particularly energetic granite" reports authority on geomancy Paul Devereux. He calls the Quoit a radioactive-interactive environment in that bursts of light, apparitions and altered states have been experienced by numerous individuals in its precincts and within its interior. In her study of the religious conceptions of the Stone Age, Rachel Levy suggests that dolmens may have been portals to the world of the dead. These prehistoric cave-like enclosures are found around the world. Their function, whether ceremonial or otherwise, is yet unknown but Devereux believes they can "tell us something about the roots of Western consciousness."

page 148

Indian Head. Washington Square Park, New York City. August 1995.

pages 151–55
A Congregation of Animal Spirits (Series #1–5). Also known as *The Balancing Rocks*. June 1995. In a small canyon in east-central Oregon there appears out of nowhere a startling array of conically shaped megaliths, each crowned with a flat stone slab that drapes over its respective pedestal. The effect is that of a petrified stone forest of strange living forms sculpted from prehistoric lava flow. Eliot Bowen told me that while photographing this lunarlike site of silent witnesses to eons of memory, he felt surrounded by strong animal spirits. Their presence was palpable and persisted throughout his experience on this remote hillside gulch. It has been written that natural healing forces proliferate on the surface of this little canyon.

page 158
Womb. Near Lake Quinault, Olympic Peninsula, Washington. September 1992.

page 162
Stonehenge. Salisbury Plain, Wiltshire, England. 1989. The literature on Stonehenge, one of the world's most impressive megalithic monuments, is massive offering a broad range of theories for its existence: temple of the Druids, observatory, stone-age computer, a memorial, place of assembly, seat of human sacrifice, solar center, locus of important rituals. The exact purpose of this magnificent Neolithic site continues to be a mystery. It is generally agreed that its construction was in several phases, the first beginning ca. 3000 B.C. Its primary form is the "trilithon," which consists of two stone pillars capped with a horizontal slab. The central trilithon rises to a height of more than 25 feet and measures 10 feet in width. To Alexander Thom, a Scot, and retired professor of engineering at Oxford University, the megalith builders were sophisticated engineers and astronomers. In *Megalithic Sites in Britain* (1967), Thom suggests that Stonehenge was at the center of a vast interlocking system of astronomical sites that methodically covered the landscape. His meticulous surveys of the monolithic landscapes together with his statistical insights have created powerful evidence for the astronomical dimensions of megalithic sites. In recent times, Stonehenge has also been regarded as a mindscape (Devereux) as well as an entirely spiritualized energy vortex.

page 168
Sea Lion. Also known as the "Blind Fiddler"; Penwith Peninsula, Cornwall, England. January 1989. The striking megalith stands 10 feet 9 inches high. It is "thickly studded with quartz . . . and is said to be a petrified Sabbath Day reveller," writes John Michel in *The Old Stones of Land's End.*

page 172
Tregeseal Circle. Penwith Peninsula, Cornwall, England. January 1989. The isolated rocky Land's End peninsula of Cornwall (now West Penwith) at the extreme western tip of England is fertile magnetic ground—the sacred land of the Druids—and host to a multitude of stone circles, cairns, tors, quoits, and megaliths associated with religious, divina-

tory, astronomical, funereal, and fertility traditions. Tregeseal Circle is one of more than 900 known stone circles throughout the British Isles.

page 180
Peak Experience. Rock Outcropping; Arches National Park, Utah. May 1993.

page 183
Wolf Emergent. Hoh Rain Forest, Olympic Peninsula, Washington. March 1995.

page 185
Hoh Gargoyle. Hoh Rain Forest, Olympic Peninsula, Washington.

page 188
Tree Angel. Hoh Rain Forest, Olympic Peninsula, Washington. March 1995.

page 191
Close Encounter. Arches National Park, Utah. June 1995.

page 196
Totem Tree (displaying rain forest canopy). Chan Chich, Belize, Central America. 1990.

page 199
Camel in Repose. Arches National Monument, Utah. June 1995.

page 204
Avenue of the Living Stones. Also known as "Avebury Avenue of Stones," West Kennet Avenue, Avebury, England. January 1989. An avenue of two parallel lines of standing stones, extending to a length of nearly 1½ miles, originally linked the south entrance of the Avebury Complex to the stone circles on Overton Hill, known as the Sanctuary. Erected probably between 2500 and 2000 B.C., the great stones exhibit contrasting characteristics—tall slim pillars alternating with shorter and broader diamond shapes—believed by some to be male and female symbols. Depending upon the eye of the beholder, a fascinating range of intriguing animal, human and mythological forms and faces has been described and reported.

pages 212–13
Boscawen-un Stone Circle (triptych). Boscawen-un Farm, Penwith Peninsula, Cornwall, England. January 1989. Considered "the most charming" of the granite and quartz Cornish stone circles, Boscawen-un consists of a ring of 19 stones with a firmly entrenched tall central pillar rising at an incline. It is considered one of the principal Gorsedd centers, or ancient bardic meeting places, in Britain. The discovery by the renowned scientist Sir Norman Lockyer of two outlying stones at Boscawen-un staking the position of sunrise in May and November strongly suggests an astronomical function of this aligned megalithic site. In his book *Stonehenge and other British Stone Monuments Astronomically Considered* (1906), Lockyer—who is considered the "father of archaeoastronomy"—describes the astronomical dimensions of the megaliths and stone circles and

identifies them as the temples and observatories of second and third B.C. ruling "astronomer-priests and priestesses." As yet, however, there is no direct archaeoastronomical evidence for this; but it is growing. It is generally conceded that the stone monuments of West Penwith were constructed some 4,000 years ago.

The Dragon Project Trust in Cornwall—whose goal has been the measurement of the earth's magnetism, its energy effects (magnetic fields, natural radiation, infra-red, visible light, ultrasound, etc.) at prehistoric sites—has confirmed in recent years that all stone circles in Britain and Wales, including many sacred megaliths across the planet, have been built within a mile of geological faulting. The Dragon discovery has identified special energy zones in the landscape especially at the megalithic and stone circle monuments. Fusion of the heavens, the earth and the mind-the spiritual, telluric and mental "scapes"—is the core element to understanding the sacred landscapes of antiquity.

page 219
Giraffe Detail. Corcovado Nature Preserve, southwest Pacific Coast of Costa Rica. February 1995.

page 222
Canine Dream. Kingston, Washington. January 1990.

page 226
Tree Knees. Kingston, Washington. April 1995.

page 230
Three Graces. Marenco Biological Reserve, southwest Pacific Coast, Costa Rica. February 1995.

page 233
Treebeard. Hoh Rain Forest, Olympic Peninsula, Washington. March 1995. Treebeard is the Elder *Ent*, the Sage Shepherd of the forest—possessed of "ages of memory" and "very penetrating" eyes—in J. R. R. Tolkien's *The Lord of the Rings*. He is tenderly portrayed by Tolkien as a "man-like, almost Troll-like, figure, at least fourteen feet high, very sturdy, with a tall head, and hardly any neck . . . the long face . . . covered with a sweeping grey beard, bushy, almost twiggy. . . ."

page 238
Pregnant Wolf Howling. Also known as "Turret Arch;" Arches National Park, Utah. June 1995. Viewed through the massive arch of North Window, Turret Arch spans 39 feet and rises to a height of 64 feet.

page 244
Yoda. Chan Chich, Belize, Central America. 1990.

page 250
Utah Pharaoh. Arches National Park, Utah. June 1995.

page 257

Mating Ritual. Also known as "Men-an-tol"; Penwith Peninsula, Western Cornwall, England. January, 1989. "Stones, rocks, monoliths, cromlechs, menhirs, etc. *become* sacred because they bear the mark of some spiritual force," writes Mircea Eliade in *Patterns in Comparative Religion.* It is thought that stones with holes have been used since time immemorial as instruments of healing, divination and fertility. The "female" and "male" stone ring and shafts of Men-an-tol were believed to be reservoirs of healing energies derived from the earth and the granite properties of the megaliths. Sick children and others seeking cures were passed through the hole three or nine times against the sun, a practice that has continued into modern times. Solar symbolism and astronomical functions have also been attributed to the significance of holed stones. In India, for example, holed stones are referred to as "gates of deliverance" from the unending cycle of birth and rebirth, says Eliade.

page 261

Cliff Faces. Columbia River Gorge, Oregon. May 1995.

page 269

Chaotic Roots. Near Lake Quinault, Olympic Peninsula, Washington. September 1992.

page 273

Eagle. Hoh Rain Forest, Olympic Peninsula, Washington. March, 1995.

FURTHER READING

In addition to the books and sources referenced in the Notes section, the following titles may be used as a guide to the significance of sacred landscapes and their impact on the evolution of human consciousness.

Albanese, Catherine L. *Nature Religion in America: From the Algonkian Indians to the New Age*. Chicago: University of Chicago Press, 1990.

Altman, Nathaniel. *Sacred Trees*. San Francisco: Sierra Club Books, 1994.

Anderson, William. *Green Man: The Archetype of Our Oneness with the Earth*. London: HarperCollins, 1990.

Awoonor, Kofi. *The Breast of the Earth*. New York: NOK Publishers International, 1975.

Bachelard, Gaston. *The Poetics of Reverie*. Trans. Daniel Russell. Boston: Beacon Press, 1971.

Bateson, Gregory. *Angels Fear: Towards an Epistemology of the Sacred*. New York: Macmillan, 1987.

———. *Mind and Nature: A Necessary Unity*. New York: E. P. Dutton, 1979.

Berman, Morris. *The Re-enchantment of the World*. Ithaca, N.Y.: Cornell University Press, 1981.

Bernbaum, Edwin. *Sacred Mountains of the World*. San Francisco: Sierra Club Books, 1990.

Berry, Thomas. *The Dream of the Earth*. San Francisco: Sierra Club Books, 1988.

Bhagavad Gita: The Song of God. Trans. Swami Prabhavananda and Christopher Isherwood. 4th ed. Hollywood, CA: Vedanta Press, 1987.

Bielecki, Tessa. *Teresa of Avila: Mystical Writings*. New York: Crossroad Publishing, 1994.

Bord, Janet, and Colin Bord. *The Secret Country*. London: Elek, 1976.

Callicott, J. Baird, and Roger T. Ames. *Nature in Asian Traditions of Thought: Essays in Environmental Philosophy*. Albany: SUNY Press, 1989.

Cook, Roger. *The Tree of Life: Image for the Cosmos*. 1974. Reprint. New York: Thames and Hudson, 1992.

Corbin, Henry. *Spiritual Body and Celestial Earth*. Trans. Nancy Pearson. Bollingen Series XCI, vol. 2. Princeton, NJ: Princeton University Press, 1977.

Cowan, James G. *The Mysteries of the Dream-Time: The Spiritual Life of Australian Aborigines*. Bridport, Dorset: Prism Press; Lindfield, NSW: Unity Press, 1989.

de Chardin, Pierre Teilhard. *The Future of Man.* New York: Harper & Row, 1969.

Devereux, Paul. *Places of Power: Secret Energies at Ancient Sites.* London: Blandford, 1990.

Fowles, John. *The Tree.* Boston: Little, Brown, 1979.

French, R. M., trans. *The Way of the Pilgrim.* New York: Harper & Row, 1954. Reprint. San Francisco: HarperSanFrancisco, 1991.

Fukuoka, Masanobu. *The Natural Way of Farming: The Theory and Practice of Green Philosophy.* Trans. Frederic P. Metreaud. Tokyo: Japan Publications, 1985.

_____. *The Road Back to Nature.* Trans. Frederic P. Metreaud. Tokyo: Japan Publications, 1987.

Heyneman, Martha. *The Breathing Cathedral: Feeling Our Way into a Living Cosmos.* San Francisco: Sierra Club Books, 1993.

Hoffman, John Floyd. *Arches National Park: An Illustrated Guide and History.* San Diego: Western Recreational Publications, 1981.

Huth, Hans. *Nature and the American: Three Centuries of Changing Attitudes.* Berkeley and Los Angeles: University of California Press, 1957; Lincoln: University of Nebraska Press, 1972.

Huxley, Francis. *The Way of the Sacred.* London: Bloomsbury Books, 1989.

Joussaume, Roger. *Dolmens for the Dead: Megalith-Building Throughout the World.* Ithaca: Cornell University Press, 1988.

Jung, C. G. *Alchemical Studies.* Trans. R. F. C. Hull. Bollingen Series XX, vol. 13. Princeton, N.J.: Princeton University Press, 1976.

Kazantzakis, Nikos. *Report to Greco.* Trans. P. A. Bien. New York: Simon & Schuster, 1965.

Levy, Rachel. *The Gate of Horn: A Study of the Religious Conceptions of the Stone Age, and Their Influence Upon European Thought.* London: Faber and Faber, 1948.

Lopez, Barry. *Arctic Dreams: Imagination and Desire in a Northern Landscape.* New York: Charles Scribner's Sons, 1986.

_____. *The Rediscovery of North America.* Lexington, Ky.: University Press of Kentucky, 1990.

Lundquist, John M. *The Temple: Meeting Place of Heaven and Earth.* New York: Thames and Hudson, 1993.

McLuhan, T. C. *Dream Tracks: The Railroad and the American Indian, 1890–1930.* New York: Harry N. Abrams, 1985.

_____. *Touch the Earth.* New York: Outerbridge and Dienstfrey, 1971. Reprint. New York: Simon & Schuster, a Touchstone Book, 1992.

_____. *The Way of the Earth: Encounters with Nature in Ancient and Contemporary Thought.* New York: Simon & Schuster, 1994.

Merton, Thomas. *The Collected Poems of Thomas Merton.* New York: New Directions, 1977.

_____. *The Seven Storey Mountain.* 1948. Reprint. New York: New American Library, a Signet Book, 1952.

Michel, John. *The Earth Spirit: Its Ways, Shrines, and Mysteries*. New York: Crossroad Publishing, 1975.

_____. *Megalithomania: Artists, Antiquarians and Archaeologists at the Old Stone Monuments*. London: Thames and Hudson, 1982.

Nasr, Seyyed Hossein. *Islamic Cosmological Doctrines: An Introduction*. Rev. ed. London: Thames and Hudson, 1978.

_____. *Man and Nature: The Spiritual Crisis of Modern Man*. 1968. Reprint. London: Unwin Paperbacks, a Mandala Book, 1976.

Novak, Barbara. *Nature and Culture: American Landscape and Painting 1825–1875*. New York: Oxford University Press, 1980.

Parlow, Anita. *A Song from Sacred Mountain*. Pine Ridge, S.D.: Oglala Lakota Legal Rights Fund, 1983.

Perlman, Michael. *The Power of Trees: The Reforesting of the Soul*. Dallas: Spring Publications, 1994.

Robins, Don. *Circles of Silence*. London: Souvenir Press, 1985.

Schama, Simon. *Landscape and Memory*. New York: Alfred A. Knopf, 1995.

Sheldrake, Rupert. *The Rebirth of Nature*. New York: Bantam, 1991.

Sherrard, Philip, ed. *The Pursuit of Greece: An Anthology*. Denise Harvey & Co., 1987.

Suzuki, Daisetz. *The Essentials of Zen Buddism: An Anthology of the Writings of Daisetz T. Suzuki*. Ed. Bernard Phillips. London: Rider and Co., 1963.

Tagore, Rabindranath. *The Religion of Man*. London: George Allen & Unwin, 1931. Reprint. Boston: Beacon Press, 1961.

Thom, Alexander. *Megalithic Sites in Britain*. Oxford: Clarendon, 1967.

van der Post, Laurens. *The Lost World of the Kalahari*. New York: William Morrow, 1958.

INDEX

Aachen cathedral, 3
abaton (inaccessible ground),
    6
Abbey, Edward, 169, 173,
    182
Abraham, 166
Adam, 166
Adams, Ansel, ix
AE, *see* Russell, George
    William
Akuropon people, 10
Allah, House of, 166–67
Altamira cave, 12
amnesia, spiritual, 69
Ananda Sonja, 253
ancestralism, 146–47
Angkor Wat, 160
animists, caves as venues for,
    11
Anlo-Ewe people, 145–47
Ape & The Whale, The
    (Novak), 127

Appalachian Mountains,
    220–21
Ararapikva (Lang), 207–9
Ardjuna Wiwaha (Kanwa), 77
Ascent of Mount Carmel (John
    of the Cross), 205
ash trees, 99
Asian Journal (Merton),
    130–31
Asoka, Emperor, 96
astronomy, ancient, 14
asvattha trees, 95
Athara Veda, 75
Athenian temples, 72
Athi Plains, 116
Australian Aborigines, 6–7,
    15, 19, 25–26, 113–14
    sand sculptures of, 160–61
Avebury, 3, 14
Awoonor, Kofi, 58–59,
    145–47
Axis, Mountain of the, 109

Ayers Rock, 7
Ayurveda, 36

Ba, Amadou Hampate, 6
Badri Narayan, 268
Balzac, Honoré de, 225, 232
Bantu, 39
banyan trees, 95, 103, 255
baobab trees, 10, 25–26
Barratt, Amy, 215
Bashō, Matsuo, 16, 29, 53,
    150
basho trees, 53
basil, 82–83
Bauls of Bengal, 258, 271
Beatific Vision, 5
Beaufort, M., 38
Bedagi, 47
beech trees, 30
Beguines, 239
Bellamy, David, 100
Bellow, Saul, 247

Benedictines, 210
Bernard of Clairvaux, Saint, 5, 30
Berry, Thomas, 220–21
Bhagavad Gita, The, 15, 94
Bielecki, Tessa, 205–6
birch trees, 99
birth rituals, 86
Black Mesa mountain range, 7
Blake, William, 11, 32, 236
Blofeld, John, 156–57, 214–15
Bodhgaya, 119–20, 242
bodhi trees, 10, 96, 119
Bowen, Eliot, 19–21
"Bridal Mysticism" (Bielecki), 205–6
Brueton, Diana, 135
Brynach, Saint, 13
Buckley, Thomas, 248–49
Buddhism, 5, 119, 156–57, 164–65, 214, 217, 242–43
 Old Sect of, 165
 trees in, 10, 29, 57, 96, 98
 see also Zen Buddhism
Bushmen, 39, 112
Butala, Sharon, 193–94

cairns, 109–10
Calaveras, North Grove at, 72
Canterbury, 28
Carmel, Mount, 205–6
Carn Ingli, 13
Carnac, 1–2
carpets, traditional Islamic, 136
Carter, Forrest, 90–91
Carthage, 163
Catherine of Siena, Saint, 4

caves, 11–12, 121, 133–34, 165
 temples in, 156–57
 under trees, 159
cedar trees, 66–67, 85
Celts, 109, 189, 202
Central Park (New York), 10
Chaco Canyon, 14
chakras, lotus, 36
Chalice Well, 2
Chang-Thang, 217
Charlemagne, 3
Chartres cathedral, 3, 160
Chauvet cave, 12
Cherokee tribe, 90–91
chestnut trees, 29
Chetan, Anand, 135
Chiang Yee, 178–79
Chilula people, 10
Chinese Eye, The (Chiang Yee), 178–79
chortens, 164–65
Christianity, 2, 48, 205–6, 210, 232, 268
Chuang Tzu, 254
cinnamon trees, 77
Civil War, 143
Clifton Beach, 252
Cloud of Unknowing, The, 17
Clutesi, George, 55
Colorado Plateau, 123
Columbus, Christopher, 105
Comes the Voyager at Last (Awoonor), 58
Communism, Chinese, 214
Confucius, 200
correlation, 14–15
Cosmic Tree, 10, 95
Cowan, James, 25, 160–61
creation myths, 34, 207
cummings, e. e., 256

Dante Alighieri, 5, 161
Darwin, Charles, 126–28, 234
Davis, Fido, 10
Day, Dorothy, 17
de Mello, Anthony, ix, 240–41
De Testimonio Animae (Tertullian), 232
deer, 174–75
Dervishes, 166
deserts, 182
Devereux, Paul, 3
dharmakaya (essence of the universe), 130
dhyana (higher stages of meditation), 218
Dine people, 7
Divine Comedy (Dante), 5
Divine Egg, 10
djel (mythological map), 160–61
Dōgen, 14
dolmens, 1
D'Orsigny Papyrus, 85
Douglas firs, 70
Druids, 101

Earth, 7–8
 numinous nature of, 64–65
Education of Little Tree, The (Carter), 90–91
Egypt, ancient, 85, 121
 hieroglyphs of, 160–61
Ehrlich, Gretel, ix, 107, 171, 176–77
Einstein, Albert, 228
Eliade, Mircea, 6, 11
Elijah, 206
elm trees, 66
Emerson, Ralph Waldo, 2, 8, 223

William Morrow & Company for material from *A Far-Off Place* by Laurens van der Post, copyright © 1974 by Laurens van der Post.

New Directions Publishing Corporation for excerpts from *The Asian Journal of Thomas Merton* by Thomas Merton, copyright © 1975 by The Trustees of the Merton Legacy Trust.

Kathleen Norris for material from *Dakota: A Spiritual Geography* by Kathleen Norris, copyright © 1993 by Kathleen Norris, published by Houghton Mifflin Company.

Barbara Novak for material from *The Ape & The Whale* by Barbara Novak, copyright © 1995 by Barbara Novak, published by Homestead Publishing.

Regina O'Melveny for an excerpt from "The Ginkgo Tree" by Regina O'Melveny, copyright © 1991 by Regina O'Melveny. Published in *The Sun*, August 1991.

Peter Owen Publishers, London, for material from *The Way and the Mountain* by Marco Pallis, copyright © 1961 by Marco Pallis.

Naveen Patnaik for material from *The Garden of Life: An Introduction to the Healing Plants of India*, by Naveen Patnaik, copyright © by Naveen Patnaik, published by Doubleday.

Penguin Books Ltd., UK, for material from *The Narrow Road to the Deep North* by Matsuo Basho, translated by Nobuyuki Yuasa, copyright © 1966 Nobuyuki Yuasa; excerpts from *The Sacred Yew* by Anand Chetan and Diane Brueton, copyright © 1994 by Anand Chetan and Diane Brueton.

Rider & Co., an imprint of Random House UK Ltd., for material from *The Way of the White Clouds* by Lama Anagarika Govinda, copyright © 1992 by Lama Anagarika Govinda.

Shambhala Publications for material from *The Wheel of Life: The Autobiography of a Western Buddhist* by John Blofeld, copyright © 1988 by John Blofeld. Reprinted by arrangement with Shambhala Publications, Inc., 300 Massachusetts Avenue, Boston, MA 02115.

Colin Smythe Limited, on behalf of the Estate of Diarmuid Russell from "Ireland Behind the Veil" by George William Russell, first published in *Universal Brotherhood*, June 1897; in March 1922 in *The Theosophical Path* (Point Loma, Calif.); in 1988 in *The Descent of the Gods: The Mystical Writings* (Part 3 of the Collected Works of G.W. Russell), Gerrards Cross, Buckinghamshire, UK.

Robert Thurman for an excerpt from an interview with the Venerable Tara Tulku, Rinpoche, "A New Dwelling," published in *Parabola*, vol. 9, no. 3, 1984.

Viking Penguin for an excerpt from *To Jerusalem and Back: A Personal Account* by Saul Bellow, copyright © 1976 by Saul Bellow. Originally published in *The New Yorker*, July 12, 1976 ("Reflections, The Middle East").

Robert Walshe for an excerpt from *Wales' Work* by Robert Walshe, copyright © 1986 by Robert Walshe, published by Ticknor & Fields.

The author has made reasonable efforts to locate and credit copyright owners. Any new or additional information in this regard may be submitted to the publisher.